FEDERAL RULES OF CIVIL PROCEDURE

With Statutory Supplement, Selected Statutes, Official Forms, Cases and Other Materials

ProCore Mastery

DISCLAIMER

This study guide provides general information about the Federal Rules of Civil Procedure. While every effort has been made to ensure accuracy, the law evolves constantly. This material should supplement, not replace, thorough legal research and professional judgment in actual practice.

TABLE OF CONTENTS

Preface

The Federal Rules of Civil Procedure represent one of the most significant legal reforms of the 20th century, transforming American civil litigation from a complex maze of technical pleading requirements into a unified, accessible system focused on resolving disputes on their merits. This study guide is designed to help law students, bar candidates, and practicing attorneys navigate the intricacies of federal civil procedure with clarity and confidence.

Civil procedure is fundamentally different from substantive law. While contracts, torts, and constitutional law deal with rights and duties, civil procedure provides the machinery for enforcing those rights. Understanding civil procedure means grasping how the legal system transforms disputes between private parties into court decisions, and ultimately, into enforceable judgments.

This guide approaches the Federal Rules not as isolated technical requirements, but as an integrated system designed to achieve the fundamental goal articulated in Rule 1: "the just, speedy, and inexpensive determination of every action and proceeding." Every rule serves this overarching purpose, and understanding this unifying principle is essential to mastering civil procedure.

HOW TO USE THIS GUIDE

This guide is organized to mirror the official Federal Rules of Civil Procedure structure while providing enhanced learning tools designed specifically for mastering civil procedure concepts.

Each rule analysis follows a consistent format:

1. Rule Text: Complete text of the rule as currently in effect
2. Core Requirements: Essential elements broken down into digestible components
3. Practical Application: Real-world scenarios showing how courts apply the rule
4. Strategic Considerations: Tactical implications for effective advocacy
5. Common Pitfalls: Frequently made errors and how to avoid them
6. Cross-References: Related rules and statutory provisions
7. Exam Focus: Key testing points for law school and bar examinations

Recommended Learning Sequence

For Law School Success

1. Week 1-2: Master Title I-II (foundations, jurisdiction, service)
2. Week 3-4: Focus on Title III (pleadings and motion practice)

3. Week 5-6: Conquer Title V (discovery rules)
4. Week 7-8: Study Title IV and VI (parties and trial procedures)
5. Week 9-10: Complete remaining titles and practice integration

For Bar Examination Preparation

1. Phase 1: Concentrate on "High-Frequency Rules" identified in each section
2. Phase 2: Practice with integrated fact patterns combining multiple rules
3. Phase 3: Review strategic decision-making scenarios
4. Phase 4: Time-pressured practice with typical bar exam formats

For Practicing Attorneys

1. Use the Quick Reference sections for immediate practical guidance
2. Focus on Strategic Considerations for tactical advantage
3. Utilize Cross-References for comprehensive rule interactions
4. Reference Common Pitfalls to avoid malpractice risks

Learning Methodology

Active Reading Approach

- Preview: Read rule headings and key requirements before detailed study
- Engage: Work through hypothetical scenarios as you read

- Review: Use chapter summaries to reinforce core concepts
- Apply: Complete practice problems to test understanding

Conceptual Integration:

- Vertical Learning: Understand how each rule fits within its Title
- Horizontal Learning: See connections between rules across different Titles
- Temporal Learning: Follow the chronological flow of litigation
- Strategic Learning: Consider procedural choices from advocate perspective

Special Features and Tools

1. Statutory Supplement Integration: Key statutory provisions (28 U.S.C. §§ 1331, 1332, 1367, etc.) are integrated into relevant rule discussions rather than relegated to appendices.
2. Case Law Synthesis: Rather than exhaustive case citations, focus is on landmark decisions that establish fundamental principles and frequently tested scenarios.
3. Local Rules Awareness: Guidance on where local district court rules commonly supplement federal rules, with examples from major districts.

Exam and Practice Preparation

1. Issue Spotting Development: Each section includes common fact patterns that trigger rule applications, helping develop the critical skill of identifying procedural issues quickly.
2. Time Management: Estimated study times for each section help allocate preparation efficiently based on complexity and testing frequency.
3. Mnemonics and Memory Aids: Strategic memory devices for complex rule requirements and numerical standards (e.g., Rule 26(f) meet and confer timing).
4. Practice Integration: Scenarios combining multiple rules reflect real-world practice where procedural issues rarely arise in isolation.

Troubleshooting Common Problems

1. "I'm overwhelmed by detail": Focus first on the "Core Requirements" and "Exam Focus" sections, then add detail gradually.
2. "I confuse similar rules": Pay special attention to cross-references that highlight distinctions.
3. "I memorize but can't apply": Spend more time with "Practical Application" sections and work through all hypothetical scenarios.

Foundations

THE ARCHITECTURE OF CIVIL LITIGATION

Civil procedure is best understood as architecture – a carefully designed framework that guides parties through the litigation process from initial dispute to final resolution. Like any well-designed building, the Federal Rules provide structural support, clear pathways, and systematic organization. This guide will help you navigate that architecture with confidence.

How to Approach This Guide

1. Understanding Over Memorization: Civil procedure rewards understanding of concepts, relationships, and strategic thinking over rote memorization. Focus on grasping why rules exist, how they interact, and what policies they serve.
2. Chronological Thinking: Unlike substantive law courses that often examine topics in isolation, civil procedure follows the natural progression of litigation. Think chronologically: What happens first? What are the prerequisites? What are the consequences of each procedural choice?
3. Strategic Perspective: Every procedural rule creates strategic opportunities and constraints. Effective lawyers don't just comply with procedures – they use

procedures as tools to advance their clients' interests while protecting against opponents' tactical moves.

The Federal Court System Context

The Federal Rules operate within a specific institutional context that shapes their application:

1. Limited Jurisdiction: Federal courts are courts of limited jurisdiction. Subject matter jurisdiction – the power to hear particular types of cases – is always the threshold inquiry. No procedural sophistication can overcome a lack of jurisdiction.
2. Federalism Considerations: Federal courts often apply state substantive law while using federal procedural rules. Understanding the Erie doctrine and the Rules Enabling Act is essential to grasping this interplay.
3. Case Management Philosophy: Modern federal practice emphasizes active judicial case management. Rule 16 conferences, discovery limitations, and mandatory disclosures reflect a philosophy of efficiency and judicial control that pervades the entire system.

Key Principles Underlying the Federal Rules

1. Notice Pleading: The Federal Rules abandoned the technical fact pleading of common law in favor of simplified notice pleading. Rule 8 requires only "a short and plain statement" that gives fair notice of claims.

This philosophical shift moves fact development from pleadings to discovery.

2. Liberal Joinder: The Rules encourage resolution of related disputes in a single action through broad joinder provisions. Rules 18-24 reflect a preference for comprehensive dispute resolution over multiple separate lawsuits.
3. Broad Discovery: Rules 26-37 establish one of the world's most expansive discovery systems, based on the principle that informed decision-making requires access to relevant information. Discovery serves truth-finding and promotes settlement by eliminating information asymmetries.
4. Proportionality: Recent amendments emphasize proportionality – discovery and case management must be proportional to the stakes, complexity, and resources involved in each case. This principle now permeates many rules.

Reading and Interpreting the Rules

1. Text and Purpose: Always start with the rule's text, but understand its purpose. Advisory Committee Notes provide invaluable insight into the drafters' intentions and the problems each rule was designed to solve.
2. Judicial Interpretation: Courts have broad discretion in applying the Federal Rules. Understanding how courts typically exercise that discretion is as important as knowing the rule's requirements.

3. Local Variations: Each federal district has local rules that supplement the Federal Rules. These local rules often address practical matters like motion practice, discovery procedures, and courtroom conduct.

Organization of This Guide

This guide follows the official organization of the Federal Rules, grouped into Titles that reflect the chronological progression of litigation:

Title I establishes the foundational principles and unified approach to civil actions.

Title II addresses case initiation – how lawsuits begin and how parties are brought before the court.

Title III covers pleadings and motions – the formal documents that define the dispute and seek court action.

Title IV examines parties – who can sue, who must be sued, and how multiple parties can be joined.

Title V details discovery – the extensive fact-gathering phase that characterizes modern litigation.

Title VI governs trials – both jury and bench trials, including the presentation of evidence and jury instructions.

Title VII addresses judgments – how courts resolve cases and the effects of those resolutions.

Title VIII covers provisional and final remedies – the tools courts use to provide effective relief.

Titles IX-XI address special proceedings, court administration, and general provisions.

Title XIII contains supplemental rules for specialized maritime and forfeiture cases.

Common Student Challenges

1. Overwhelming Detail: The Federal Rules contain extensive detail that can obscure underlying principles. Focus first on understanding concepts, then master specific requirements.
2. Artificial Isolation: Don't study rules in isolation. Civil procedure is a system where rules interact and influence each other. Understanding these interactions is crucial.
3. Passive Learning: Civil procedure rewards active engagement. Work through hypothetical problems, trace the procedural steps in real cases, and think strategically about procedural choices.
4. Federal/State Confusion: Keep federal and state practice separate in your mind. This guide focuses on federal practice, which often differs significantly from state procedures.

Title I - Scope of Rules; Form of Action

Title I establishes the foundational principles governing all federal civil litigation by defining the scope, purpose, and unified structure of the Federal Rules of Civil Procedure. These two concise but powerful rules transformed American civil practice in 1938 by abolishing the rigid distinction between law and equity that had plagued the legal system for centuries. Rule 1 articulates the overarching philosophy of federal procedure, emphasizing efficiency, fairness, and accessibility, while Rule 2 creates the unified procedural framework that allows all civil claims to proceed under a single set of rules regardless of their historical legal or equitable nature.

RULE 1. SCOPE AND PURPOSE

"These rules govern the procedure in all civil actions and proceedings in the United States district courts, except as stated in Rule 81. They should be construed, administered, and employed by the court and the parties to secure the just, speedy, and inexpensive determination of every action and proceeding."

Core Requirements

Rule 1 establishes the foundational mandate for all federal civil procedure. Three core principles guide every procedural decision: justice, speed, and economy. Courts must balance these sometimes competing values when interpreting other rules or exercising discretion.

Universal Application: The Federal Rules apply to all civil proceedings in federal district courts unless specifically excluded by Rule 81. This includes diversity cases applying state substantive law and federal question cases applying federal substantive law.

Interpretive Mandate: Rule 1 requires courts and attorneys to interpret all other rules in light of these three objectives. When rule language is ambiguous, courts should choose the interpretation that best serves the just, speedy, and inexpensive resolution of disputes.

Historical Context

Before 1938, federal courts followed the Conformity Act, which required them to use the procedural rules of the state where they sat. This created a patchwork of different procedures across federal districts. Additionally, law and equity maintained separate procedural systems with different pleading requirements, discovery rules, and remedial powers.

The Federal Rules revolutionized American civil procedure by creating uniform national standards and merging law and equity into a single "civil action." Rule 1 represents this philosophical shift from technical procedural compliance toward substance-focused dispute resolution.

Practical Application

1. Judicial Discretion: Courts regularly cite Rule 1 when exercising discretion in case management decisions. For example, judges may extend deadlines, allow liberal amendment of pleadings, or modify discovery schedules when doing so serves the rule's underlying purposes.
2. Rule Interpretation: When procedural rules conflict or create ambiguity, Rule 1 provides the interpretive framework. Courts favor constructions that promote fair resolution over those that create technical obstacles.
3. Attorney Conduct: Rule 1 influences how lawyers approach procedural decisions. Effective advocates frame procedural arguments in terms of fairness, efficiency, and cost-effectiveness rather than mere technical compliance.

The Three-Part Mandate

1. Just Determination: Justice requires fair procedures that give all parties adequate opportunity to present their cases. This includes proper notice, reasonable time for response, and meaningful access to relevant information through discovery.
2. Speedy Determination: Speed demands efficient case management without sacrificing fairness. Courts should

eliminate unnecessary delay while preserving essential procedural protections. The rule encourages settlement, alternative dispute resolution, and streamlined procedures where appropriate.

3. Inexpensive Determination: Economy requires proportionality between the costs of litigation and the stakes involved. Procedures should not impose burdens that exceed the value of the dispute or prevent parties from accessing the court system.

Balancing Competing Values

These three objectives sometimes conflict. Thorough discovery serves justice but may compromise speed and economy. Expedited procedures may reduce costs but risk unfairness if parties lack adequate preparation time. Rule 1 requires courts and attorneys to balance these values contextually, considering the specific circumstances of each case.

Strategic Considerations

1. Motion Practice: Attorneys should frame procedural arguments in Rule 1 terms. Instead of merely citing technical rule violations, explain how granting or denying relief serves or undermines just, speedy, and inexpensive resolution.
2. Case Management: Judges use Rule 1 to justify active case management. Lawyers should anticipate judicial intervention in discovery disputes, scheduling conflicts, and procedural inefficiencies.

3. Settlement Promotion: Rule 1 supports judicial efforts to encourage settlement through mandatory conferences, alternative dispute resolution, and cost-shifting mechanisms.

Common Examination Issues

1. Rule Application: Students must understand that Rule 1 provides the framework for interpreting all other rules. When analyzing procedural problems, consider how different interpretations serve or undermine Rule 1's objectives.
2. Discretionary Decisions: Courts have broad discretion in applying procedural rules, but that discretion is constrained by Rule 1's mandate. Analyze judicial decisions in terms of how they balance justice, speed, and economy.
3. Policy Analysis: Law school examinations often ask students to evaluate procedural reforms or rule changes. Use Rule 1's framework to assess whether proposed changes would improve the system's ability to resolve disputes justly, speedily, and inexpensively.

RULE 2. ONE FORM OF ACTION

"There is one form of action which is the civil action."

Core Requirements

Rule 2 eliminates the historical distinction between legal and equitable proceedings. All civil cases in federal court proceed under the unified "civil action" format, regardless of whether they seek legal remedies (damages) or equitable remedies (injunctions, specific performance).

Single Procedural Framework: Plaintiffs no longer must choose between law and equity courts. The same pleading requirements, discovery rules, and trial procedures apply whether seeking monetary damages, injunctive relief, or both.

Unified Remedy System: Courts can grant both legal and equitable relief in the same action. A contract dispute might result in both damages for past breach and an injunction preventing future violations.

Historical Background

Under English common law, legal and equitable claims required separate courts with different procedures. Law courts provided monetary damages through jury trials with strict pleading requirements. Equity courts granted injunctions and other discretionary relief through bench trials with more flexible procedures.

American courts initially maintained this distinction. The Federal Rules' merger of law and equity represented a fundamental reform, eliminating procedural barriers that prevented comprehensive dispute resolution.

Practical Application

1. Pleading Flexibility: Plaintiffs can include both legal and equitable claims in a single complaint without choosing between different procedural tracks. A breach of contract case might seek both damages and specific performance.
2. Remedial Options: Courts have full remedial power in every civil action. Judges can award damages, injunctions, declaratory relief, restitution, and other remedies as justice requires.
3. Jury Trial Rights: The merger affects but does not eliminate the constitutional right to jury trial. Legal claims retain jury trial rights, while equitable claims are tried to the court. When both types of claims appear in one case, courts must carefully manage trial procedures to preserve jury rights for appropriate issues.

Strategic Implications

1. Comprehensive Pleading: Lawyers should include all available claims and requested relief in the initial complaint. The unified system allows complete dispute resolution without multiple lawsuits.
2. Discovery Advantages: Single-action treatment means one discovery process covers all claims, reducing costs and eliminating duplicative fact-gathering.
3. Settlement Leverage: The availability of both legal and equitable remedies provides additional settlement leverage and negotiation flexibility.

Jury Trial Considerations

Rule 2's merger creates complexity for jury trial rights. Courts must determine which issues require jury determination (legal issues) and which are for the court alone (equitable issues).

1. Issue Segregation: When legal and equitable claims involve common factual issues, courts often try legal issues first to preserve jury rights, then decide equitable issues based on the jury's factual findings.
2. Clean-up Doctrine: Courts may decide legal issues even in primarily equitable cases when the legal issues are incidental to the main equitable relief sought.

Common Pitfalls

1. Remedy Confusion: Students sometimes believe Rule 2 eliminates substantive differences between legal and equitable remedies. The merger affects procedure only. Substantive requirements for different remedies remain distinct.
2. Jury Trial Oversimplification: The rule does not mean jury trial is available for all claims. Constitutional and statutory jury rights depend on the nature of the claim and remedy sought, not the procedural framework.

Examination Focus

1. Historical Understanding: Understand what problems Rule 2 solved and how it changed federal practice. This context helps explain many other rule features.

2. Remedial Analysis: When analyzing case problems, consider what types of relief are available and how Rule 2 enables comprehensive resolution.
3. Procedure vs. Substance: Distinguish between procedural unification (which Rule 2 accomplishes) and substantive law differences (which remain unchanged).

Connection to Other Rules

Rule 2 enables the broad joinder provisions in Rules 18-24. Without procedural unification, the flexible joinder of claims and parties would be impossible.

The rule also supports Rule 8's simplified pleading requirements. Notice pleading works because courts have full remedial power to craft appropriate relief regardless of how claims are characterized in the pleadings.

Modern Significance

While taken for granted today, Rule 2 represents one of the Federal Rules' most significant innovations. The unified civil action enables:

1. Efficient Dispute Resolution: Complete resolution of related disputes in a single proceeding
2. Flexible Case Management: Courts can adapt procedures to each case's specific needs
3. Comprehensive Relief: Full range of remedial options available in every case

Practice Applications

1. Complaint Drafting: Include all potential claims and remedies rather than limiting options through narrow pleading choices.
2. Case Strategy: Develop litigation strategies that leverage the full range of available remedies, not just traditional damages.
3. Client Counseling: Advise clients about the complete spectrum of relief available through the unified civil action system.

Title II - Commencing an Action; Service of Process, Pleadings, Motions, and Orders

Title II governs the critical initial phase of federal litigation, establishing procedures for commencing lawsuits and ensuring proper notice to all parties. These rules address fundamental due process requirements by creating uniform standards for starting federal cases and providing defendants with adequate notice of legal proceedings against them. From the simple filing requirement that commences an action under Rule 3 to the comprehensive service procedures in Rule 4, this title balances efficiency with constitutional protections. The rules also establish essential timing requirements and notice procedures that affect statute of limitations, personal jurisdiction, and case management throughout the litigation process.

RULE 3. COMMENCING AN ACTION

"A civil action is commenced by filing a complaint with the court."

Core Requirements

Rule 3 establishes the precise moment when federal civil litigation begins. Filing the complaint with the court clerk commences the action, regardless of whether the defendant has been served. This simple rule has profound implications for statutes of limitations, jurisdictional deadlines, and case management.

Filing Requirement: The complaint must be physically or electronically filed with the appropriate court clerk. Merely preparing the complaint or serving it on the defendant without court filing does not commence the action.

Immediate Effect: Once filed, the action exists for all legal purposes. The case receives a docket number, the statute of limitations typically stops running, and the court gains authority to manage the proceedings.

Service Independence: Rule 3 separates commencement from service of process. The action begins when filed, but defendants need not be served until later (subject to Rule 4's time limits).

Practical Application

1. Statute of Limitations: Rule 3 typically stops the statute of limitations from running, preserving the plaintiff's right to sue even if service occurs weeks or months later. However, some federal statutes and state laws may require actual service for limitations purposes.
2. Jurisdictional Deadlines: Certain statutory deadlines run from the commencement date. For example, removal rights under 28 U.S.C. § 1446 begin when defendants are served, but some administrative appeal deadlines may run from filing.

3. Case Management: Courts begin managing cases from the filing date. Many districts issue automatic scheduling orders and set case management deadlines based on the Rule 3 commencement date.

Strategic Considerations

1. Emergency Filing: When facing an imminent statute of limitations deadline, Rule 3 allows plaintiffs to commence the action by filing, buying time to perfect service under Rule 4Forum Selection: The filing date may affect forum selection in cases where multiple potential forums exist. First-filed rules in multidistrict litigation often turn on Rule 3 commencement dates.
2. Discovery Timeline: Since case management deadlines often run from filing, early filing can provide more discovery time, though courts may adjust schedules based on actual service dates.

Common Pitfalls

1. Electronic Filing Issues: Technical failures during electronic filing can prevent commencement. Attorneys must ensure successful submission and receipt of confirmation.
2. Incomplete Complaints: Filing an incomplete or defective complaint still commences the action under Rule 3, but may require amendment under Rule 15.

State Law Variations

While Rule 3 governs federal procedure, state statutes of limitations may have different commencement requirements. Some states require service for limitations purposes, creating Erie doctrine complications in diversity cases.

RULE 4. SUMMONS

Rule 4 is extensive, containing detailed provisions for summons content, issuance, service methods, and time limits.

Core Requirements

Rule 4 governs the summons process, which provides defendants with formal notice of the lawsuit and the court's assertion of personal jurisdiction. The summons must accompany the complaint when served on defendants.

Summons Content (Rule 4(a)): The summons must:

- Name the court and parties
- Direct the defendant to appear and defend within specified time
- State the consequences of failing to appear
- Be signed by the clerk and bear the court's seal

Issuance (Rule 4(b)): Upon filing the complaint, the plaintiff may present a summons to the clerk for signature and seal. The plaintiff is responsible for service.

Service Methods: Rule 4 provides multiple service options depending on the type of defendant and location.

Service on Individuals (Rule 4(e))

1. Personal Service: Direct delivery to the defendant personally, anywhere within the United States.
2. Dwelling Service: Leaving copies at the defendant's usual place of residence with a person of suitable age and discretion who resides there.
3. Agent Service: Service upon an authorized agent.
4. State Law Methods: Service may also be made under the law of the state where the district court sits or where service is made.

Service on Corporations and Entities (Rule 4(h))

Service on domestic or foreign corporations requires delivery to:

- An officer, managing agent, or general agent
- Any other agent authorized by appointment or law
- Following state law methods where the district court sits

Waiver of Service (Rule 4(d))

Rule 4(d) encourages cost-saving through a waiver system:

1. Waiver Request: Plaintiffs may request waiver by mailing notice and waiver forms to defendants with prepaid return envelope.
2. Benefits of Waiving: Defendants who waive service get 60 days to answer (instead of 21 days) and avoid service costs.
3. Consequences of Refusing: Defendants who refuse reasonable waiver requests must pay service costs unless they show good cause.
4. Cannot Waive Personal Jurisdiction: Waiver of service does not waive objections to personal jurisdiction or venue.

Service Outside the United States (Rule 4(f))

International service requires:

- Methods permitted by international agreement (such as Hague Service Convention)
- Methods permitted by foreign country's law
- Personal service (unless prohibited by foreign law)
- Mail service (if not prohibited)
- Court-ordered alternative methods

Time Limits (Rule 4(m))

1. 90-Day Deadline: Service must be completed within 90 days after filing the complaint.
2. Extension Available: Courts must extend time for good cause and may extend time even without good cause shown.
3. Dismissal Consequences: Failure to serve within the deadline (including extensions) results in dismissal without prejudice unless the plaintiff shows good cause.

Proof of Service (Rule 4(l))

Service must be proved by:

- Server's affidavit stating time, place, and method of service
- For waiver, the signed waiver form
- Court order when service was made by court order

Strategic Considerations

Waiver Requests: In straightforward cases with cooperative defendants, waiver requests save time and money while providing additional response time.

Service Planning: Complex service situations (corporate entities, international service, evasive defendants) require advance planning to meet the 90-day deadline.

Personal Jurisdiction: Effective service establishes personal jurisdiction over defendants, making service method selection crucial for jurisdictional purposes.

Common Examination Issues

1. Service Defects: Students must identify improper service methods and understand waiver effects.
2. Time Calculations: The 90-day service deadline and its relationship to Rule 6 time computation rules frequently appear on exams.
3. Personal Jurisdiction Connection: Understanding how service methods relate to personal jurisdiction requirements is essential.

RULE 4.1. SERVING OTHER PROCESS

"Unless a statute expressly provides otherwise, process, other than a summons or a subpoena, must be served by a United States marshal or deputy marshal or by a person specially appointed for that purpose."

Core Requirements

Rule 4.1 governs service of court orders and other process besides summons. This includes temporary restraining orders, preliminary injunctions, contempt orders, and other court directives requiring immediate compliance.

Marshal Service: Default requirement for service by U.S. Marshals ensures reliable, official service for important court orders.

Special Appointment: Courts may appoint special process servers when marshal service is unavailable or inappropriate.

Statutory Exceptions: Specific statutes may provide different service requirements for particular types of process.

Practical Applications

1. Emergency Orders: TROs and preliminary injunctions often require immediate service to be effective, making marshal service valuable for its reliability and speed.
2. Contempt Proceedings: Service of contempt orders by marshals provides official authority and documentation important for enforcement.
3. Cost Considerations: Marshal service involves fees, but ensures proper service for important court orders where reliability outweighs cost concerns.

RULE 5. SERVING AND FILING PLEADINGS AND OTHER PAPERS

Rule 5 requires service of pleadings and other papers on all parties after the original complaint.

Core Requirements

Rule 5 establishes the fundamental requirement that parties must serve copies of all filed papers on opposing parties, ensuring that litigation proceeds with full notice to all participants.

Service Requirement (Rule 5(a)): After the original complaint, every pleading, motion, and other paper must be served on every party.

Service Methods (Rule 5(b)): Papers may be served by:

- Personal delivery
- Mailing to last known address
- Electronic means if consented to
- Other court-approved methods

Filing Requirement (Rule 5(d)): Papers must be filed with the court before or promptly after service, unless court rules provide otherwise.

Electronic Service and Filing

Most federal courts now require electronic filing and permit electronic service:

1. CM/ECF System: Electronic filing through the court's Case Management/Electronic Case Files system automatically serves registered users.

2. Consent Required: Electronic service generally requires party consent, though some courts mandate electronic service for represented parties.
3. Paper Service Exception: Non-registered parties and pro se litigants may require traditional paper service.

Certificate of Service

Every served paper must include a certificate of service stating:

- Date of service
- Method of service
- Parties served
- Attorney signature

Strategic Considerations

1. Service Timing: Service and filing deadlines may differ under local rules, affecting motion practice timing.
2. Electronic Advantages: Electronic service provides immediate delivery and automatic documentation, reducing service disputes.
3. Pro Se Complications: Cases involving self-represented parties require careful attention to service methods and proof requirements.

RULE 5.1. CONSTITUTIONAL CHALLENGE TO A STATUTE

Rule 5.1 requires notice to government entities when parties challenge the constitutionality of federal or state statutes.

Core Requirements

When challenging statute constitutionality, parties must provide notice to appropriate government attorneys, allowing governmental defense of the challenged law.

Federal Statute Challenges: Notice must be served on the United States Attorney General when challenging federal statute validity.

State Statute Challenges: Notice must be served on the state attorney general when challenging state statute validity in federal court.

Timing: Notice must be served promptly after filing the constitutional challenge, whether in initial pleadings or later motions.

Notice Content

The notice must identify:

- The constitutional challenge being raised
- The statute or regulation being challenged
- The specific constitutional provision allegedly violated

Practical Application

1. Government Intervention: Notice allows government attorneys to intervene and defend the statute's constitutionality, ensuring adequate representation of governmental interests.
2. Procedural Compliance: Failure to provide required notice may result in sanctions or case delays while proper notice is provided.
3. Strategic Timing: Early notice allows government participation in case management and discovery planning.

RULE 5.2. PRIVACY PROTECTION FOR FILINGS MADE WITH THE COURT

Rule 5.2 requires redaction of sensitive personal information from court filings to protect privacy.

Core Requirements

Rule 5.2 addresses privacy concerns in an era of electronic filing and online case access by requiring redaction of sensitive personal information.

Required Redactions: Unless otherwise required by law, parties must redact:

- Social Security numbers (show only last four digits)
- Financial account numbers (show only last four digits)
- Birth dates (show only year)

- Minor children's names (use initials only)

Complete Restriction: Never include home addresses in pleadings except when required for jurisdictional purposes.

Practical Application

- Electronic Filing Impact: With court records available online, privacy protection has become crucial for preventing identity theft and protecting personal information.
- Compliance Responsibility: Attorneys and parties bear responsibility for proper redaction before filing documents.
- Sealed Filing Option: When complete personal information is necessary, parties may seek to file documents under seal with court approval.

Strategic Considerations

- Discovery Documents: Privacy rules apply to discovery materials filed with the court, requiring careful review before submission.
- Settlement Agreements: Filed settlement agreements must comply with privacy requirements while preserving essential terms.
- Administrative Efficiency: Proper initial redaction prevents the need for later document withdrawal and refiling.

RULE 6. COMPUTING AND EXTENDING TIME; TIME FOR MOTION PAPERS

Rule 6 provides uniform methods for calculating deadlines and requirements for motion papers.

Time Computation (Rule 6(a))

Rule 6 establishes precise methods for calculating procedural deadlines, preventing disputes about due dates.

Counting Method:

- Exclude the triggering event day
- Include the deadline day unless it falls on weekend/holiday
- When deadline falls on weekend/holiday, extend to next business day
- Weekend/Holiday Rule: If the last day falls on Saturday, Sunday, or legal holiday, the deadline extends to the next business day.
- "Business Day" Definition: Days when the court clerk's office is open for business.

Extending Time (Rule 6(b))

Courts have broad discretion to extend deadlines with important limitations:

1. Before Expiration: Courts may extend deadlines for good cause with or without motion or notice.

2. After Expiration: Courts may extend expired deadlines only for good cause and if the failure to act resulted from excusable neglect.
3. Non-Extendable Deadlines: Some deadlines cannot be extended, including those for post-trial motions under Rules 50, 52, and 59.

Motion Papers Timing (Rule 6(c) and (d))

1. Service Timing: Written motions must be served at least 14 days before hearing date unless court rules provide otherwise or the motion is for summary judgment, preliminary injunction, or other specified motions with longer periods.
2. Response Time: Opposing parties typically have time to respond before hearings, with specific periods set by local rules or court order.

Strategic Applications

1. Deadline Management: Effective lawyers calculate all deadlines immediately upon receiving court orders or scheduling conferences.
2. Extension Requests: Good cause standards require showing reasonable justification and diligent effort to meet original deadlines.
3. Emergency Motions: Some situations justify shortened notice periods with court approval for urgent matters.

Common Pitfalls

1. Calendar Confusion: Misunderstanding business day calculations leads to missed deadlines and potential sanctions.
2. Extension Assumptions: Assuming courts will grant extensions without proper justification creates malpractice risks.
3. Local Rule Variations: Different districts may have varying requirements for motion practice timing and notice periods.

Examination Focus

1. Time Calculation Problems: Law school exams frequently test Rule 6 deadline calculations with various weekend and holiday scenarios.
2. Extension Standards: Understanding the difference between pre-expiration and post-expiration extension standards is crucial for exam analysis.
3. Integration with Other Rules: Rule 6 timing provisions affect nearly all other procedural deadlines, making integration essential for comprehensive analysis.

TITLE III - PLEADINGS AND MOTIONS

Title III represents the strategic heart of federal civil procedure, where cases are shaped, narrowed, and often resolved before reaching trial. These ten rules govern how parties present their claims and defenses, challenge opponent assertions, and seek court intervention through motions. Understanding these provisions is essential for effective litigation practice, as pleading defects can prove fatal to otherwise meritorious claims, while skillful motion practice can dispose of weak cases efficiently and cost-effectively.

RULE 7. PLEADINGS ALLOWED; FORM OF MOTIONS AND OTHER PAPERS

"Only these pleadings are allowed: (1) a complaint; (2) an answer to a complaint; (3) an answer to a counterclaim designated as a counterclaim; (4) an answer to a crossclaim; (5) a third-party complaint; (6) an answer to a third-party complaint; and (7) if the court orders one, a reply to an answer."

Core Requirements

Rule 7 establishes the exclusive list of permitted pleadings in federal court, creating a streamlined system that prevents the proliferative pleading practices that plagued earlier procedural systems. This limitation promotes efficiency while ensuring adequate opportunity for claim and defense presentation.

Permitted Pleadings: The rule creates a closed list of seven allowable pleadings. No other pleading types may be filed without specific court permission, eliminating historical complications from demurrers, replications, and other archaic pleading forms.

Complaint Foundation: The complaint initiates the case and establishes the factual and legal framework for all subsequent proceedings. It must satisfy Rules 8, 9, and 10 requirements while providing fair notice of claims.

Answer Obligations: Defendants must respond to complaints with answers that admit, deny, or claim insufficient knowledge about each allegation. Failure to respond appropriately may result in deemed admissions.

Reply Limitations: Replies to answers are permitted only when courts specifically order them, preventing unnecessary pleading exchanges that delay case progress.

Motion Requirements (Rule 7(b))

Rule 7(b) governs motion practice, establishing uniform standards for requesting court action:

1. Writing Requirement: All motions must be in writing unless made during hearings or trials. This ensures clear record development and prevents misunderstandings about requests.

2. Grounds Specification: Motions must state with particularity the grounds for relief and the specific relief sought. Vague or conclusory motion practice violates Rule 7 standards.
3. Supporting Materials: While Rule 7 does not mandate supporting briefs, most courts require legal memoranda supporting non-routine motions. Local rules often specify brief length and format requirements.

Practical Applications

1. Pleading Strategy: The limited pleading system requires careful initial drafting, as opportunities for clarification through additional pleadings are restricted. Complaints must anticipate likely defenses and address them preemptively.
2. Motion Practice Excellence: Effective motion writing requires precision in identifying legal grounds and requested relief. Courts appreciate motions that clearly articulate issues and proposed resolutions.
3. Discovery Integration: Since replies are rarely allowed, parties must structure initial pleadings to accommodate expected discovery disputes and motion practice.

Strategic Considerations

1. Complaint Comprehensiveness: Given reply limitations, complaints should address anticipated defenses and provide sufficient detail to survive motion practice.

2. Answer Tactics: Defendants can use answers strategically to narrow disputed issues while preserving affirmative defenses and counterclaims.
3. Motion Timing: Understanding local motion practice schedules helps attorneys coordinate discovery deadlines with dispositive motion filing dates.

Common Pitfalls

1. Unauthorized Pleadings: Attempting to file sur-replies, duplicative motions, or other non-permitted papers wastes time and may result in sanctions.
2. Motion Defects: Failing to specify relief sought or providing inadequate grounds statements can result in motion denial without reaching the merits.
3. Local Rule Compliance: Motion format requirements vary significantly between districts, making local rule familiarity essential for effective practice.

RULE 7.1. DISCLOSURE STATEMENT

"A nongovernmental corporate party must file 2 disclosure statements: (1) a corporate disclosure statement identifying any parent corporation and any publicly held corporation owning 10% or more of its stock; and (2) a disclosure statement identifying any persons, associations of persons, firms, partnerships, or corporations that have a financial interest in the outcome of the litigation."

Core Requirements

Rule 7.1 promotes judicial transparency by requiring corporate parties to disclose ownership structures and financial interests that might create conflicts of interest for judges.

Corporate Structure Disclosure: Corporations must reveal parent companies and any entity owning ten percent or more of their stock, allowing judges to identify potential conflicts with their financial holdings.

Financial Interest Disclosure: The broader financial interest statement captures entities that might benefit from litigation outcomes, including litigation funding arrangements and profit-sharing agreements.

Filing Timeline: Initial disclosure statements must be filed with first pleadings, with supplemental statements filed when circumstances change.

Practical Applications

1. Judicial Recusal: These disclosures help judges identify conflicts requiring recusal, preventing appealable errors and ensuring case integrity.
2. Third-Party Funding: Modern litigation funding arrangements may trigger disclosure requirements when funders have financial stakes in case outcomes.
3. Complex Corporate Structures: Multi-layered corporate ownership requires careful analysis to identify all entities meeting disclosure thresholds.

Strategic Considerations

1. Complete Disclosure: Under-disclosure risks sanctions and potential case reversal if conflicts are later discovered.
2. Ongoing Obligations: Corporate ownership changes during litigation may require supplemental disclosure statements.
3. Litigation Planning: Disclosure requirements may influence case strategy when corporate structure changes could benefit litigation positioning.

RULE 8. GENERAL RULES OF PLEADING

"(a) Claim for Relief. A pleading that states a claim for relief must contain: (1) a short and plain statement of the grounds for the court's jurisdiction; (2) a short and plain statement of the claim showing that the pleader is entitled to relief; and (3) a demand for the relief sought."

Core Requirements

Rule 8 establishes the foundational pleading standards for federal courts, emphasizing notice pleading over the technical fact pleading required under earlier systems. The rule balances fair notice to defendants with litigation efficiency.

Jurisdictional Statement (Rule 8(a)(1)): Every complaint must include a concise statement establishing the court's authority to hear the case. This typically involves citing specific jurisdictional statutes and alleging facts supporting federal question or diversity jurisdiction.

Claim Statement (Rule 8(a)(2)): The claim statement must be "short and plain" while "showing that the pleader is entitled to relief." This standard requires more than bare legal conclusions but less than detailed evidentiary proof.

Demand for Relief (Rule 8(a)(3)): The prayer for relief specifies monetary damages, injunctive relief, or other remedies sought. While not limiting recovery, the demand helps define case scope and discovery parameters.

Plausibility Standard

Post-Twombly and Iqbal, Rule 8 requires factual allegations that make claims plausible rather than merely possible:

1. Factual Content: Complaints must contain sufficient factual matter to allow reasonable inference that defendants are liable for alleged misconduct.
2. Legal Conclusion Distinction: While legal conclusions may be included, they cannot substitute for factual allegations supporting claims.
3. Context-Specific Analysis: Plausibility depends on case-specific circumstances, requiring attorneys to craft allegations that make relief plausible given the particular legal and factual context.

Defenses and Responses (Rule 8(b))

Rule 8(b) governs answer requirements, establishing the framework for defendant responses:

1. Response Options: Defendants must admit, deny, or state insufficient knowledge about each allegation. Evasive responses may be treated as admissions.
2. Good Faith Standard: Denials must be made in good faith based on reasonable belief about the truth of allegations.
3. Partial Admissions: When allegations contain both true and false elements, defendants must specify which portions they admit and deny.

Affirmative Defenses (Rule 8(c))

Rule 8(c) requires defendants to raise affirmative defenses in their answers or risk waiving them:

1. Enumerated Defenses: The rule lists nineteen common affirmative defenses including statute of limitations, fraud, res judicata, and statute of frauds.
2. Waiver Consequences: Failure to raise affirmative defenses in answers typically results in waiver, though courts may allow amendments in appropriate circumstances.
3. Burden Implications: Affirmative defenses typically shift the burden of proof to defendants, making proper identification crucial for trial preparation.

Strategic Applications

1. Complaint Drafting: Effective complaints anticipate likely Rule 12(b)(6) challenges by including sufficient factual detail to meet plausibility standards while remaining concise.
2. Answer Strategy: Defense attorneys must carefully review complaints to identify all viable affirmative defenses and ensure proper assertion to avoid waiver.
3. Discovery Planning: Rule 8 allegations define discovery scope, making strategic pleading decisions important for controlling litigation costs and timeline.

Common Pitfalls

1. Conclusory Pleading: Relying on legal conclusions without supporting facts violates post-Iqbal pleading standards and invites motion practice.
2. Defense Waiver: Inadequate attention to affirmative defense requirements can eliminate viable defenses and compromise settlement negotiations.
3. Jurisdictional Defects: Insufficient jurisdictional allegations can result in dismissal and potential statute of limitations problems when refiling.

RULE 9. PLEADING SPECIAL MATTERS

Rule 9 establishes heightened pleading requirements for specific types of claims, departing from Rule 8's general notice pleading standard where policy considerations demand greater specificity.

Fraud Claims (Rule 9(b))

Rule 9(b) requires fraud allegations to meet heightened "particularity" standards while allowing general pleading for knowledge and intent elements:

1. Particularity Requirement: Fraud pleadings must specify the who, what, when, where, and how of alleged fraudulent conduct. Conclusory allegations of fraud fail to meet Rule 9(b) standards.
2. Intent Exception: While fraudulent intent may be alleged generally, courts increasingly require some factual basis supporting intent allegations to meet plausibility standards.
3. Reliance Elements: When fraud claims require reliance proof, complaints should identify specific misrepresentations and explain how plaintiffs relied on them.
4. Securities Fraud: Federal securities cases must comply with both Rule 9(b) and heightened pleading requirements under the Private Securities Litigation Reform Act, creating additional complexity.

Special Damages (Rule 9(g))

Rule 9(g) requires specific pleading of special damages, which include losses that do not naturally flow from defendant's conduct:

1. Natural vs. Special: General damages flow naturally from wrongful conduct (such as property damage from negligent driving), while special damages require specific allegation (such as lost business profits).
2. Specificity Standard: Special damages must be pleaded with sufficient detail to provide fair notice and enable meaningful response.
3. Calculation Basis: While precise dollar amounts are not required, pleadings should provide reasonable basis for damages calculations.

Conditions Precedent (Rule 9(c))

When contract performance depends on conditions precedent, Rule 9(c) allows general allegations:

1. General Allegation: Plaintiffs may generally allege that all conditions precedent have been performed or excused without detailed specificity.
2. Defendant Response: Defendants who wish to contest condition precedent performance must specifically deny such allegations in their answers.
3. Burden Allocation: This pleading approach efficiently allocates burdens while ensuring adequate notice about disputed performance issues.

Practical Applications

1. Fraud Case Strategy: Successful fraud pleadings require intensive factual investigation before filing to meet particularity requirements and avoid sanctions.
2. Damages Documentation: Early damages calculation and documentation supports Rule 9(g) compliance and provides foundation for settlement negotiations.
3. Contract Claim Efficiency: Rule 9(c) streamlines contract litigation by avoiding unnecessary condition precedent disputes when performance is undisputed.

Strategic Considerations

1. Investigation Investment: Rule 9(b) cases require greater pre-filing investigation, affecting litigation budgets and filing timelines.
2. Amendment Opportunities: Courts are more reluctant to allow fraud claim amendments, making initial pleading accuracy crucial.
3. Settlement Leverage: Well-pleaded special damages enhance settlement value by demonstrating damages scope and calculation methodology.

Common Examination Issues

1. Fraud Specificity: Bar exams frequently test whether fraud allegations meet Rule 9(b) particularity requirements.

2. Special Damages Identification: Students must distinguish between general and special damages to determine pleading requirements.
3. PSLRA Integration: Securities fraud questions often combine Rule 9(b) with statutory heightened pleading requirements.

RULE 10. FORM OF PLEADINGS

"Every pleading must have a caption with the court's name, a title, a file number, and a Rule 7(a) designation. The title of the complaint must name all the parties; other pleadings need not name all parties unless the court orders it."

Core Requirements

Rule 10 establishes uniform formatting standards that promote clarity and administrative efficiency across the federal court system.

Caption Requirements (Rule 10(a)): Every pleading must contain a complete caption identifying the court, case title, file number, and pleading type. Captions provide essential case identification and docket management information.

Party Identification: Complaints must name all parties in the title, while subsequent pleadings may use abbreviated forms like "Plaintiff v. Defendant, et al." unless courts require complete party identification.

Paragraph Structure (Rule 10(b)): Rule 10 requires numbered paragraphs with single claims or defenses per paragraph, facilitating clear responses and streamlined fact development.

Formatting Standards

1. Professional Appearance: While Rule 10 does not mandate specific fonts or margins, professional pleading appearance enhances credibility and demonstrates attorney competence.
2. Electronic Filing Compliance: Modern electronic filing systems impose additional formatting requirements beyond Rule 10 minimums, including PDF format and metadata requirements.
3. Local Rule Variations: Districts often supplement Rule 10 with detailed formatting requirements covering everything from font size to signature blocks.

Practical Applications

1. Document Identification: Proper captions ensure accurate docket entries and prevent filing confusion in courts managing thousands of cases simultaneously.
2. Response Facilitation: Numbered paragraphs enable precise responses and streamline discovery disputes by providing clear reference points for specific allegations.
3. Administrative Efficiency: Standardized formatting reduces clerk processing time and minimizes administrative errors in case management.

Strategic Considerations

1. Professional Standards: High-quality pleading format enhances attorney credibility and demonstrates attention to detail that may influence judicial perceptions.
2. Amendment Planning: Well-organized initial pleadings facilitate future amendments by providing clear structural frameworks for additional allegations.
3. Multi-Party Management: Complex cases benefit from careful caption and organization decisions that accommodate multiple parties and claims.

RULE 11. SIGNING PLEADINGS, MOTIONS, AND OTHER PAPERS; REPRESENTATIONS TO THE COURT; SANCTIONS

"Every pleading, written motion, and other paper must be signed by at least one attorney of record in the attorney's name—or by a party personally if the party is unrepresented."

Core Requirements

Rule 11 creates a critical accountability mechanism requiring attorneys and parties to certify the good faith basis for court filings. This rule serves as a gatekeeper against frivolous litigation while protecting attorneys who conduct reasonable pre-filing investigations.

Signature Requirements (Rule 11(a)): Every court filing must be signed by an attorney or unrepresented party. Electronic signatures satisfy this requirement in courts using electronic filing systems.

Attorney Responsibility: Signatures constitute personal certifications by individual attorneys, creating professional liability even when other attorneys in the firm participate in case preparation.

Certification Standards (Rule 11(b)): By signing, attorneys certify that:

- The filing is not for improper purposes (harassment, delay, unnecessary cost increase)
- Legal contentions are warranted by existing law or good faith argument for law modification
- Factual allegations have evidentiary support or will likely have support after reasonable discovery opportunity
- Denials are warranted on evidence or reasonably based on belief or lack of information

Sanctions Framework (Rule 11(c))

Rule 11 provides structured sanctions procedures protecting against frivolous litigation while ensuring due process:

1. Motion Requirements: Sanctions motions must be served on the challenged party but not filed immediately. The 21-day safe harbor period allows voluntary withdrawal of challenged papers.

2. Safe Harbor Protection: Parties may avoid sanctions by withdrawing or correcting challenged filings within 21 days after service of the sanctions motion.
3. Sanction Types: Courts may impose monetary sanctions, non-monetary sanctions (such as continuing education requirements), or other appropriate measures designed to deter repetition and compensate for expenses.
4. Limit on Monetary Sanctions: Sanctions must be limited to what suffices to deter repetition and may not exceed expenses caused by the violation.

Good Faith Standard

Rule 11's good faith requirement creates objective and subjective components:

1. Reasonable Investigation: Attorneys must conduct factual and legal research reasonable under the circumstances before filing.
2. Objective Basis: Claims and defenses must have reasonable foundation in law and fact, measured by professional competence standards.
3. Subjective Honesty: Attorneys must honestly believe in the validity of their contentions based on their investigation and legal analysis.

Practical Applications

1. Pre-Filing Investigation: Rule 11 requires substantial factual investigation before filing fraud claims, complex commercial disputes, or cases involving technical subject matter.
2. Legal Research Standards: Attorneys must research controlling law and recent developments before advancing legal theories, particularly in rapidly evolving areas.
3. Discovery Limitations: Rule 11 prevents fishing expedition discovery by requiring factual foundations for allegations before extensive fact-finding begins.

Strategic Considerations

1. Documentation Practices: Maintaining investigation files and legal research memoranda helps demonstrate Rule 11 compliance and provides sanctions defense materials.
2. Client Communication: Attorneys should document client information sources and verify factual representations to establish good faith investigation foundations.
3. Settlement Timing: Rule 11 concerns may influence settlement negotiations when parties question case foundations or defense viability.

Sanctions Defense

When facing Rule 11 challenges, effective responses include:

1. Investigation Documentation: Demonstrating reasonable pre-filing investigation through witness interviews, document review, and legal research.
2. Legal Precedent: Identifying supporting case law and legal authorities that provide reasonable foundation for contentions.
3. Factual Support: Presenting available evidence supporting allegations and explaining reasonable expectations for additional discovery development.

Common Pitfalls

1. Insufficient Investigation: Rushing to file without adequate factual development creates Rule 11 vulnerability and potential malpractice exposure.
2. Frivolous Arguments: Advancing legal theories without reasonable foundation or ignoring clearly controlling adverse authority violates certification standards.
3. Improper Purpose: Using litigation for harassment, delay, or strategic advantage unrelated to legal merit constitutes sanctionable conduct.

Bar Examination Focus

1. Certification Analysis: Exams often require analysis of whether specific attorney conduct meets Rule 11 standards.

2. Sanctions Procedures: Understanding the 21-day safe harbor and sanctions motion requirements appears frequently in procedural analysis questions.
3. Integration with Other Rules: Rule 11 interacts with discovery sanctions (Rule 37) and other professional responsibility requirements.

RULE 12. DEFENSES AND OBJECTIONS; WHEN AND HOW PRESENTED; MOTION FOR JUDGMENT ON THE PLEADINGS; CONSOLIDATING MOTIONS; WAIVING DEFENSES; PRETRIAL HEARING

Rule 12 governs the presentation of defenses and objections, creating a sophisticated framework for testing pleading sufficiency and jurisdictional adequacy before costly discovery begins.

Core Requirements

Rule 12 provides defendants with multiple tools for challenging complaints while establishing waiver rules that encourage efficient motion practice and prevent dilatory tactics.

Defense Presentation Options (Rule 12(a)): Defendants may present defenses through answers or pre-answer motions. The choice affects timing, strategy, and waiver implications.

Motion Types Available: Rule 12 permits seven categories of motions, each serving distinct purposes in litigation management:

- Rule 12(b)(1): Lack of subject matter jurisdiction
- Rule 12(b)(2): Lack of personal jurisdiction
- Rule 12(b)(3): Improper venue
- Rule 12(b)(4): Insufficient process
- Rule 12(b)(5): Insufficient service of process
- Rule 12(b)(6): Failure to state a claim upon which relief can be granted
- Rule 12(b)(7): Failure to join a party under Rule 19

Subject Matter Jurisdiction Challenges (Rule 12(b)(1))

Subject matter jurisdiction challenges receive special treatment because courts cannot proceed without proper authority:

1. Non-Waivable Defense: Unlike other Rule 12 defenses, subject matter jurisdiction objections cannot be waived and may be raised at any time during proceedings.
2. Court Obligation: Courts must examine subject matter jurisdiction independently, even when parties do not challenge it.
3. Dismissal Standard: Dismissal for lack of subject matter jurisdiction is without prejudice, allowing refiling in courts with proper jurisdiction.
4. Factual vs. Facial Challenges: Courts may consider evidence beyond the complaint when resolving factual disputes about jurisdictional elements.

Personal Jurisdiction and Venue (Rules 12(b)(2) and 12(b)(3))

Personal jurisdiction and venue challenges protect defendants from inconvenient or improper forums:

1. Personal Jurisdiction Defense: Challenges court authority over the defendant's person, requiring analysis of constitutional due process and state long-arm statute requirements.
2. Venue Defense: Challenges whether the chosen district is proper under applicable venue statutes, focusing on conduct location and defendant residence.
3. Waiver Rules: Both defenses are waived if not raised in first responsive pleading or Rule 12 motion, encouraging prompt challenge and resolution.

Process Challenges (Rules 12(b)(4) and 12(b)(5))

Process and service defects challenge the mechanics of providing defendant notice:

1. Insufficient Process: Attacks defects in the summons itself, such as improper court seal, incorrect party names, or missing required information.
2. Insufficient Service: Challenges the method or manner of service, including failure to follow Rule 4 requirements or applicable state law service methods.

3. Waiver Vulnerability: Both defenses are easily waived and may be cured by proper service, making them less powerful than jurisdictional challenges.

Motion to Dismiss for Failure to State a Claim (Rule 12(b)(6))

The Rule 12(b)(6) motion tests whether complaints state legally cognizable claims:

1. Pleading Adequacy: Courts examine whether allegations, accepted as true, establish legal claims entitling plaintiffs to relief.
2. Plausibility Standard: Post-Iqbal analysis requires factual allegations making claims plausible rather than merely possible.
3. Limited Scope: Courts generally consider only complaint allegations, though may consider documents incorporated by reference and matters subject to judicial notice.
4. Conversion Issues: If parties present materials outside the pleadings, courts may convert Rule 12(b)(6) motions to summary judgment motions under Rule 56.

Failure to Join Required Parties (Rule 12(b)(7))

Rule 12(b)(7) challenges inadequate party joinder when necessary parties are absent:

1. Rule 19 Integration: This defense requires analysis of Rule 19 required joinder standards, examining whether absent parties are necessary and indispensable.
2. Feasibility Considerations: Courts consider whether joinder is feasible given jurisdiction and venue limitations affecting absent parties.
3. Dismissal vs. Joinder: Successful Rule 12(b)(7) motions may result in dismissal or court orders requiring party joinder when feasible.

Motion for Judgment on the Pleadings (Rule 12(c))

Rule 12(c) motions seek judgment after pleadings close but before trial:

1. Timing Requirements: These motions are available only after pleadings are closed, typically after answers are filed.
2. Standard Application: Courts apply the same standard as Rule 12(b)(6) motions, accepting well-pleaded allegations as true and drawing inferences favorable to non-movants.
3. Strategic Utility: Rule 12(c) motions are useful when answers reveal legal theories insufficient to support defenses or counterclaims.

Consolidation Requirements (Rule 12(g))

Rule 12(g) promotes efficiency by requiring consolidation of available Rule 12 motions:

1. Motion Consolidation: Parties must include all available Rule 12 defenses in their first Rule 12 motion or risk waiving them.
2. Exception for Rule 12(h)(2) Defenses: Failure to state a claim, failure to join required parties, and lack of subject matter jurisdiction may be raised later.
3. Strategic Implications: Consolidation requirements force comprehensive motion strategy decisions early in litigation.

Waiver Provisions (Rule 12(h))

Rule 12(h) creates a hierarchical waiver structure protecting core jurisdictional principles while encouraging prompt challenge of technical defects:

1. Immediate Waiver (Rule 12(h)(1)): Personal jurisdiction, venue, process, and service defects are waived if not raised in first responsive pleading or Rule 12 motion.
2. Answer Deadline Waiver (Rule 12(h)(2)): Failure to state a claim and failure to join required parties are waived if not raised in pleadings or Rule 12 motion before answer.
3. Never Waived (Rule 12(h)(3)): Subject matter jurisdiction objections may be raised at any time and must be considered by courts sua sponte.

Strategic Applications

1. Motion Timing Strategy: Defense counsel must decide whether to file Rule 12 motions or proceed directly to answer based on motion strength and client objectives.
2. Discovery Considerations: Successful Rule 12 motions can eliminate costly discovery, while unsuccessful motions may delay discovery and increase litigation costs.
3. Settlement Leverage: Strong Rule 12 motions provide settlement leverage while weak motions may strengthen plaintiff positions.

Practical Considerations

1. Local Practice Variations: Districts vary significantly in Rule 12 motion scheduling, briefing requirements, and hearing procedures.
2. Oral Argument: While not required, oral argument on Rule 12 motions can be valuable for complex legal issues or when written briefs require clarification.
3. Appeal Timing: Rule 12 dismissals may be immediately appealable if final, affecting litigation timeline and strategy decisions.

Common Pitfalls

1. Consolidation Failures: Failing to consolidate available Rule 12 defenses results in waiver of non-included defenses.

2. Premature Filing: Filing Rule 12(c) motions before pleadings close or Rule 12(b)(6) motions before investigating factual development opportunities.
3. Waiver Oversights: Inadequate attention to waiver rules can eliminate viable defenses and compromise case positioning.

Examination Focus

1. Waiver Analysis: Law school and bar exams extensively test Rule 12 waiver provisions and their application to various defense timing scenarios.
2. Motion Standards: Understanding the relationship between Rule 12(b)(6) standards and summary judgment requirements is crucial for examination success.
3. Strategic Decision-Making: Exams often require analysis of whether defendants should file Rule 12 motions or proceed directly to answers in given factual scenarios.

RULE 13. COUNTERCLAIM AND CROSSCLAIM

"(a) Compulsory Counterclaim. A pleading must state as a counterclaim any claim that—at the time of its service—the pleader has against an opposing party if the claim: (1) arises out of the transaction or occurrence that is the subject matter of the opposing party's claim; and (2) does not require adding another party over whom the court cannot acquire jurisdiction."

Core Requirements

Rule 13 manages related claims between parties through counterclaims against opposing parties and crossclaims against co-parties, promoting judicial efficiency while protecting claim presentation rights.

Compulsory Counterclaims (Rule 13(a)): Defendants must raise counterclaims that arise from the same transaction or occurrence as plaintiff's claims or risk losing them forever due to res judicata principles.

Transaction or Occurrence Test: Courts apply logical relationship tests examining whether claims share common factual or legal foundations, even when specific facts differ.

Jurisdictional Requirements: Compulsory counterclaims must not require joinder of parties beyond the court's jurisdictional reach, providing practical limitations on mandatory assertion.

Waiver Consequences: Failure to assert compulsory counterclaims in answers results in permanent waiver through res judicata, making identification crucial for defense strategy.

Permissive Counterclaims (Rule 13(b))

Rule 13(b) allows assertion of unrelated counterclaims without mandatory waiver consequences:

1. Unrelated Claims: Counterclaims not arising from the same transaction or occurrence may be asserted at

defendant's option without waiver consequences if omitted.

2. Jurisdictional Foundation: Permissive counterclaims require independent jurisdictional basis, as supplemental jurisdiction typically does not extend to unrelated claims.
3. Strategic Flexibility: Defendants may choose whether to assert permissive counterclaims based on litigation strategy, settlement prospects, and forum preferences.

Crossclaims (Rule 13(g))

Crossclaims allow claims between co-parties (co-defendants or co-plaintiffs):

1. Transaction Relationship: Crossclaims must arise from the same transaction or occurrence as the original action or involve property that is the subject matter of the original action.
2. Optional Nature: Unlike compulsory counterclaims, crossclaims are always permissive and carry no waiver consequences when omitted.
3. Indemnity Applications: Crossclaims frequently involve indemnity or contribution claims when multiple defendants share potential liability.

Supplemental Jurisdiction Impact

Supplemental jurisdiction under 28 U.S.C. § 1367 significantly affects Rule 13 practice:

1. Compulsory Counterclaim Coverage: Supplemental jurisdiction typically extends to compulsory counterclaims, eliminating independent federal jurisdiction requirements.
2. Permissive Counterclaim Limitations: Unrelated permissive counterclaims usually require independent federal jurisdiction, limiting assertion options in diversity cases.
3. Crossclaim Support: Related crossclaims typically qualify for supplemental jurisdiction when they meet transaction or occurrence requirements.

Strategic Applications

1. Claim Packaging: Plaintiffs should consider potential counterclaims when structuring complaints to avoid creating favorable counterclaim opportunities.
2. Defense Integration: Defendants must identify all related claims early in litigation to comply with compulsory counterclaim requirements and preserve strategic options.
3. Settlement Leverage: Counterclaims provide settlement leverage and may offset damage exposure while complicating plaintiff case management.

Timing Considerations

1. Amendment Rights: Rule 15 amendment standards apply to counterclaim and crossclaim assertions, with liberal amendment policies early in litigation.

2. Discovery Scope: Counterclaims and crossclaims expand discovery scope, affecting case complexity and litigation costs.
3. Trial Management: Multiple claims between various parties create trial management challenges requiring careful court scheduling and jury instruction coordination.

Practical Applications

1. Transactional Analysis: Attorneys must carefully analyze factual relationships between claims to determine compulsory counterclaim obligations.
2. Client Counseling: Defendants need comprehensive counseling about related claims to avoid inadvertent waiver of valuable counterclaims.
3. Case Planning: Early identification of potential counterclaims and crossclaims affects discovery planning, motion strategy, and settlement negotiations.

Common Pitfalls

1. Waiver Oversights: Failing to identify and assert compulsory counterclaims results in permanent loss of related claims.
2. Jurisdictional Assumptions: Assuming supplemental jurisdiction extends to all counterclaims without analyzing transaction relationship and jurisdictional statutes.

3. Timing Confusion: Misunderstanding when counterclaims must be asserted versus when they may be added through amendment.

Examination Focus

1. Transaction or Occurrence Analysis: Exams frequently test ability to determine whether claims arise from the same transaction or occurrence for compulsory counterclaim purposes.
2. Waiver Consequences: Understanding permanent waiver effects of failing to assert compulsory counterclaims is essential for exam success.
3. Jurisdictional Integration: Questions often combine Rule 13 analysis with supplemental jurisdiction and diversity jurisdiction requirements.

RULE 14. THIRD-PARTY PRACTICE

"A defending party may, as third-party plaintiff, serve a summons and complaint on a nonparty who is or may be liable to it for all or part of the claim against it."

Core Requirements

Rule 14 enables defendants to bring third parties into litigation when those parties may be liable for some or all of the claims against the original defendants, promoting comprehensive dispute resolution in single proceedings.

Impleader Rights: Defendants may implead third parties who are potentially liable to defendants for plaintiffs' claims through indemnity, contribution, subrogation, or other liability-shifting theories.

Timing Requirements: Third-party complaints may be filed without court permission within 14 days after serving the original answer. Later impleader requires court permission with good cause showing.

Jurisdictional Foundation: Third-party claims typically qualify for supplemental jurisdiction under 28 U.S.C. § 1367 when they arise from common factual foundations.

Liability Theories Supporting Impleader

1. Indemnity Claims: Third parties who are contractually or legally obligated to protect defendants from liability exposure provide classic impleader foundations.
2. Contribution Claims: When multiple parties share potential liability, defendants may implead co-tortfeasors to ensure proportional responsibility allocation.
3. Subrogation Rights: Insurance coverage or other subrogation relationships may support third-party practice when coverage obligations exist.
4. Derivative Liability: Employment relationships, agency arrangements, and similar derivative liability theories often justify impleader practice.

Permissible Third-Party Claims

Rule 14 permits broad claim presentation once third parties are properly joined:

1. Third-Party Defendant Claims: Third-party defendants may assert defenses against both original plaintiffs and third-party plaintiffs.
2. Plaintiff Claims: Original plaintiffs may assert claims against third-party defendants when claims arise from the same transaction or occurrence.
3. Additional Third Parties: Third-party defendants may implead additional parties following the same standards applied to original defendants.

Strategic Applications

1. Comprehensive Resolution: Impleader enables resolution of all related liability issues in single proceedings, reducing duplicative litigation and inconsistent judgments.
2. Settlement Leverage: Third-party practice affects settlement dynamics by bringing additional parties and insurance coverage into negotiations.
3. Discovery Efficiency: Consolidated discovery among all potentially liable parties reduces costs and prevents duplicative fact-finding.

Timing and Procedural Strategy

1. Early Impleader Advantages: Filing third-party complaints within the 14-day window avoids seeking court permission and potential delay.
2. Discovery Coordination: Third-party practice affects discovery scheduling, as additional parties need time to investigate claims and develop defenses.
3. Motion Practice Impact: Rule 12 motions by third-party defendants may challenge both the original complaint and third-party complaint, creating complex motion coordination requirements.

Court Discretion in Impleader

1. Severance Authority: Courts may sever third-party claims when they complicate the original action or create jury confusion about primary liability issues.
2. Case Management: Complex third-party practice may require separate discovery tracks, bifurcated trials, or other management tools to prevent prejudice to original parties.
3. Efficiency Analysis: Courts balance comprehensive dispute resolution benefits against potential delay and complexity when evaluating impleader motions.

Jurisdictional Considerations

1. Supplemental Jurisdiction: Third-party claims typically qualify for supplemental jurisdiction when they arise

from common operative facts, eliminating independent federal jurisdiction requirements.

2. Personal Jurisdiction: Third-party defendants must be subject to personal jurisdiction in the forum, which may limit impleader options in some cases.
3. Venue Impact: Third-party practice does not create new venue rights, as venue is determined by the original action's requirements.

Common Pitfalls

1. Timing Delays: Waiting beyond the 14-day window creates additional procedural hurdles and potential court rejection of untimely impleader attempts.
2. Liability Theory Confusion: Impleader requires that third parties be liable to defendants, not independently liable to plaintiffs for the same conduct.
3. Jurisdictional Oversights: Assuming supplemental jurisdiction applies without analyzing the relationship between claims and constitutional limitations.

Examination Focus

1. Liability Relationship Analysis: Exams test ability to distinguish between proper impleader relationships and independent third-party liability to plaintiffs.
2. Timing Requirements: Understanding the 14-day window and permission requirements for later impleader appears regularly in procedural analysis.

3. Jurisdictional Integration: Questions often combine Rule 14 analysis with supplemental jurisdiction and personal jurisdiction requirements.

RULE 15. AMENDED AND SUPPLEMENTAL PLEADINGS

"(a) Amendments Before Trial. (1) Amending as a Matter of Course. A party may amend its pleading once as a matter of course within: (A) 21 days after serving it, or (B) if the pleading is one to which a responsive pleading is required, 21 days after service of a responsive pleading or 21 days after service of a motion under Rule 12(b), (e), or (f), whichever is earlier."

Core Requirements

Rule 15 reflects federal courts' liberal amendment philosophy, encouraging resolution on the merits rather than pleading technicalities while providing appropriate protection against prejudicial delay and procedural abuse.

Amendment as of Right (Rule 15(a)(1)): Parties may amend pleadings once without court permission within specified time periods, promoting efficient correction of pleading defects.

Responsive Pleading Trigger: When pleadings require responses, the amendment window runs from service of the response or qualifying motion, whichever occurs earlier.

Court Permission Standard (Rule 15(a)(2)): After the "as of right" period expires, amendments require court permission, which should be "freely given when justice so requires."

Liberal Amendment Policy

Rule 15 embodies federal procedure's preference for resolving cases on their merits:

1. Justice Standard: Courts should permit amendments unless they cause undue delay, bad faith, dilatory motive, repeated failure to cure deficiencies, or prejudice to opposing parties.
2. Futility Exception: Courts may deny amendment motions when proposed amendments would be futile because they fail to state viable claims or would be immediately dismissed.
3. Relation Back Benefits: Successful amendments that relate back to original pleadings avoid statute of limitations problems, encouraging prompt case development.

Relation Back Doctrine (Rule 15(c))

Rule 15(c) allows amended pleadings to relate back to original filing dates under specific circumstances:

1. Claim Relation Back (Rule 15(c)(1)(B)): Amendments adding claims relate back when they arise from the same conduct, transaction, or occurrence as original claims.

2. Party Changes (Rule 15(c)(1)(C)): Amendments changing parties relate back when new parties received adequate notice and knew or should have known they would have been sued but for naming mistakes.
3. Notice Requirements: Relation back for party changes requires that new parties received notice within the Rule 4(m) service period, protecting statute of limitations policies.

Supplemental Pleadings (Rule 15(d))

Rule 15(d) permits addition of claims based on events occurring after original pleading service:

1. Post-Pleading Events: Supplemental pleadings address conduct occurring after the original pleading, expanding case scope to include related subsequent events.
2. Court Permission: All supplemental pleadings require court permission, with courts considering prejudice, efficiency, and case management factors.
3. Strategic Applications: Supplemental pleadings enable parties to address ongoing conduct or new developments that strengthen original claims or defenses.

Amendment Strategy

1. Early Amendment Benefits: Amending as of right avoids briefing requirements and court permission delays while preserving strategic flexibility.

2. Discovery Timing: Amendment timing affects discovery schedules, as new claims may require additional fact-finding and expert witness development.
3. Settlement Impact: Amendments can strengthen or weaken settlement positions depending on claim strength and damage scope changes.

Practical Applications

1. Pleading Improvement: Rule 15 encourages attorneys to strengthen pleadings through factual development and legal research after initial filing.
2. Claim Development: Discovery often reveals additional claims or stronger factual foundations supporting amendment motions.
3. Defense Enhancement: Defendants may amend answers to add newly discovered affirmative defenses or strengthen existing ones.

Common Pitfalls

1. Timing Miscalculations: Misunderstanding amendment timing requirements can eliminate as-of-right opportunities and create unnecessary court permission requirements.
2. Prejudice Creation: Delayed amendments that require extensive additional discovery or trial postponement may be denied for prejudice reasons.

3. Futility Failures: Proposing amendments that fail to cure known pleading defects wastes resources and may result in sanctions.

Examination Focus

1. Timing Analysis: Exams frequently test understanding of as-of-right amendment periods and their interaction with motion practice timing.
2. Relation Back Application: Questions often require analysis of whether proposed amendments meet relation back requirements for statute of limitations purposes.
3. Court Discretion Standards: Understanding factors courts consider when evaluating amendment motions under the "justice so requires" standard.

RULE 16. PRETRIAL CONFERENCES; SCHEDULING; MANAGEMENT

"(a) Purposes of a Pretrial Conference. The court may order the parties to appear before it for a conference to consider: (1) expediting disposition of the action; (2) establishing early and continuing control so that the case will not be protracted because of lack of management..."

Core Requirements

Rule 16 empowers courts with comprehensive case management authority, transforming federal judges from passive arbiters to active litigation managers responsible for controlling case pace, scope, and resource allocation.

Scheduling Orders (Rule 16(b)): Courts must issue scheduling orders in most cases setting deadlines for joinder of parties, amendment of pleadings, completion of discovery, and filing of motions.

Scheduling Conference Authority: Judges may require scheduling conferences to establish case timelines, discuss discovery scope, and address anticipated procedural issues.

Management Tools: Rule 16 provides extensive judicial tools for controlling litigation pace, costs, and complexity through ongoing supervision.

Scheduling Order Requirements

1. Mandatory Deadlines: Scheduling orders must establish deadlines for completing discovery, filing dispositive motions, and amending pleadings.
2. Amendment Standards: After scheduling order deadlines pass, amendments require showing "good cause" for deadline modification in addition to Rule 15 standards.
3. Binding Effect: Scheduling orders bind parties and courts absent good cause modifications, creating predictable litigation timelines.

4. Local Variations: Districts often have standard scheduling order forms incorporating local practice requirements and typical case management approaches.

Pretrial Conference Types

1. Initial Conferences: Early conferences establish case parameters, discovery plans, and scheduling frameworks while addressing preliminary procedural issues.
2. Status Conferences: Periodic status conferences monitor case progress, resolve discovery disputes, and adjust scheduling as needed.
3. Final Pretrial Conferences: Final conferences immediately before trial address evidentiary issues, witness lists, and jury instruction disputes.
4. Settlement Conferences: Courts may order settlement conferences to explore resolution opportunities with judicial assistance or appointed mediators.

Case Management Authority

1. Discovery Control: Rule 16 enables courts to limit discovery scope, sequence, and timing to prevent abuse while ensuring adequate fact development.
2. Motion Scheduling: Courts may establish motion filing deadlines and hearing schedules that coordinate with discovery completion and trial preparation.
3. Settlement Encouragement: Judicial case management includes settlement facilitation through conferences,

mediation orders, and other alternative dispute resolution requirements.

Good Cause Standards

1. Deadline Modification: Changing scheduling order deadlines requires good cause showings, typically involving circumstances beyond party control or changed case circumstances.
2. Burden Allocation: Moving parties bear the burden of demonstrating good cause, with courts considering prejudice to opposing parties and case management efficiency.
3. Discovery Extensions: Discovery deadline modifications require showing diligent discovery efforts and justification for additional time needs.

Sanctions Authority (Rule 16(f))

1. Conference Attendance: Courts may sanction attorneys or parties who fail to attend required conferences or participate in good faith.
2. Order Violations: Violating scheduling orders or case management directives may result in monetary sanctions, adverse evidentiary rulings, or other penalties.
3. Preparation Requirements: Conference participants must be prepared to discuss case status, settlement prospects, and scheduling issues.

Strategic Applications

1. Early Planning: Effective case management begins with comprehensive discovery planning and realistic scheduling discussions during initial conferences.
2. Deadline Management: Understanding court scheduling preferences and typical case timelines helps attorneys plan effective litigation strategies.
3. Settlement Positioning: Case management conferences provide opportunities to demonstrate case strength and explore settlement possibilities.

Practical Considerations

1. Local Practice Knowledge: District-specific case management practices significantly affect litigation experience, making local rule familiarity essential.
2. Resource Planning: Scheduling orders establish litigation budgeting parameters, affecting client counseling and fee arrangement decisions.
3. Trial Preparation: Final pretrial conferences require extensive preparation including witness coordination, exhibit organization, and jury instruction drafting.

Common Pitfalls

1. Deadline Assumptions: Assuming scheduling deadlines can be easily modified without good cause creates malpractice risks and client prejudice.

2. Conference Preparation: Inadequate conference preparation wastes judicial resources and may result in unfavorable scheduling decisions.
3. Order Compliance: Failing to comply with case management orders can result in sanctions and adverse case positioning.

Integration with Other Rules

1. Discovery Coordination: Rule 16 scheduling integrates with discovery rules (Rules 26-37) to create comprehensive case development frameworks.
2. Motion Practice: Scheduling orders affect Rule 12 and Rule 56 motion timing, requiring coordination between pleading challenges and case management deadlines.
3. Trial Preparation: Final pretrial orders often incorporate requirements from trial rules (Rules 38-53), creating comprehensive trial preparation frameworks.

Modern Developments

1. Electronic Case Management: Many courts use electronic case management systems that integrate with Rule 16 requirements for automated scheduling and deadline tracking.
2. Alternative Dispute Resolution: Rule 16 increasingly incorporates ADR requirements including mandatory mediation and early neutral evaluation programs.

3. Efficiency Initiatives: Courts implement various efficiency measures through Rule 16 authority, including discovery limitations, motion practice restrictions, and expedited trial settings.

Examination Applications

1. Case Management Analysis: Exams may require analysis of appropriate scheduling decisions and case management strategies for complex litigation scenarios.
2. Good Cause Standards: Understanding factors courts consider when evaluating deadline modification requests is essential for practice-oriented questions.
3. Sanctions Analysis: Questions may address appropriate sanctions for case management violations and their relationship to other rule-based sanctions.

TITLE IV - PARTIES

Title IV governs who can sue and be sued in federal court, how multiple claims and parties can be combined in a single action, and when parties can join ongoing litigation. These rules balance efficiency through consolidated litigation against fairness to individual parties. Understanding party rules is essential for strategic case planning, managing complex litigation, and avoiding procedural traps that can derail otherwise meritorious claims.

RULE 17. PLAINTIFF AND DEFENDANT; CAPACITY; PUBLIC OFFICERS

"(a) Real Party in Interest. An action must be prosecuted in the name of the real party in interest..."

"(b) Capacity to Sue or Be Sued. Capacity to sue or be sued is determined as follows: (1) for an individual who is not acting in a representative capacity, by the law of the individual's domicile; (2) for a corporation, by the law under which it was organized..."

Core Requirements

Rule 17 ensures that lawsuits are brought by parties who have the legal right to enforce the claims and against parties who can be held legally responsible.

Real Party in Interest (Rule 17(a)): The person who actually owns the claim must bring the lawsuit. This prevents situations where someone without legal standing attempts to prosecute another's rights.

- Assignment Rights: When claims are assigned, the assignee typically becomes the real party in interest
- Insurance Subrogation: Insurers who pay claims often become real parties in interest through subrogation
- Trust Situations: Trustees sue on behalf of beneficiaries but in their own names as real parties

Capacity Requirements (Rule 17(b)): Legal capacity to sue depends on applicable law:

- Individuals: Governed by domicile state law
- Corporations: Governed by state of incorporation
- Partnerships: Governed by state where partnership was formed
- Federal Entities: Governed by federal law

Practical Applications

1. Standing Analysis: Rule 17(a) overlaps with constitutional standing requirements but focuses on who holds the legal claim rather than constitutional injury requirements.
2. Curative Measures: When wrong parties file suit, Rule 17(a) allows substitution of proper parties without dismissing the action if done timely.

3. Representative Suits: Executors, administrators, guardians, and other representatives sue in their representative capacity for parties who cannot sue directly.

Strategic Considerations

1. Early Verification: Attorneys must verify client authority to bring claims before filing to avoid Rule 17 challenges.
2. Insurance Coordination: In cases involving insurance, determining whether the insured or insurer is the real party in interest affects case strategy and settlement authority.
3. Corporate Verification: Ensuring corporate plaintiffs exist and are in good standing prevents capacity challenges that can delay litigation.

Common Examination Issues

1. Assignment Scenarios: Students must identify who becomes the real party in interest when claims are assigned or transferred.
2. Capacity Defects: Understanding how capacity defects can be cured and the timing requirements for such corrections.
3. Representative Actions: Distinguishing between proper representative capacity and improper attempts to sue on another's behalf.

RULE 18. JOINDER OF CLAIMS

"(a) In General. A party asserting a claim, counterclaim, crossclaim, or third-party claim may join, as independent or alternative claims, as many claims as it has against an opposing party."

Core Requirements

Rule 18 provides virtually unlimited claim joinder, allowing parties to resolve all disputes between them in a single action. The rule promotes judicial efficiency while protecting parties' rights to present complete cases.

Unlimited Joinder: Parties may join any number of claims against opposing parties, regardless of whether the claims are:

- Related or unrelated
- Legal or equitable
- Similar in nature or completely different
- Arising from the same transaction or separate events

No Relationship Required: Unlike party joinder rules, Rule 18 imposes no requirement that joined claims be related to each other or arise from common facts.

Permissive Nature: Rule 18 permits but does not require claim joinder. Parties may choose to bring separate actions for strategic or practical reasons.

Jurisdictional Considerations

1. Subject Matter Jurisdiction: Each joined claim must satisfy federal subject matter jurisdiction requirements or qualify for supplemental jurisdiction under 28 U.S.C. § 1367.
2. Personal Jurisdiction: The court must have personal jurisdiction over defendants for each claim, though different jurisdictional bases may support different claims.
3. Venue: Joined claims must satisfy venue requirements, though venue is typically proper if it supports the main claim.

Supplemental Jurisdiction Analysis

1. Related Claims: Claims arising from the same transaction or occurrence typically qualify for supplemental jurisdiction even without independent federal jurisdiction.
2. Unrelated Claims: Completely unrelated claims require independent federal jurisdiction unless they fall within supplemental jurisdiction's broad scope.
3. Diversity Limitations: In diversity cases, supplemental jurisdiction has specific limitations for claims by plaintiffs against non-diverse parties.

Strategic Applications

1. Efficiency Benefits: Joining related claims avoids duplicative discovery, witnesses, and legal arguments while ensuring consistent factual findings.
2. Settlement Leverage: Multiple claims against the same defendant can provide additional negotiation leverage and settlement options.
3. Res Judicata Protection: Joining related claims prevents later preclusion arguments about claim splitting and ensures complete resolution.

Practical Limitations

1. Jury Confusion: Joining unrelated claims may confuse juries and complicate trial management.
2. Discovery Complexity: Multiple unrelated claims can expand discovery scope and increase litigation costs.
3. Settlement Complications: Different claims may have different settlement values and timing considerations.

Common Examination Issues

1. Supplemental Jurisdiction: Students must analyze whether joined claims require independent jurisdiction or qualify for supplemental jurisdiction.
2. Strategic Analysis: Exams often require evaluation of whether claim joinder is advisable given efficiency and complexity considerations.

RULE 19. REQUIRED JOINDER OF PARTIES

"(a) Persons Required to Be Joined if Feasible... (1) in that person's absence, the court cannot accord complete relief among existing parties; or (2) that person claims an interest relating to the subject of the action..."

Core Requirements

Rule 19 addresses situations where additional parties are so essential to fair adjudication that the case cannot proceed without them. The rule balances the need for complete dispute resolution against practical limitations on party joinder.

Required Joinder Analysis (Three-Step Process):

a) Determine if absentees are required parties under Rule 19(a)
b) Assess whether joinder is feasible under Rule 19(a)(1)
c) If joinder is not feasible, decide whether to proceed without them or dismiss under Rule 19(b)

Required Party Standards (Rule 19(a)):

a) Complete Relief Standard: Parties whose absence prevents complete relief among existing parties must be joined if feasible.
b) Practical Impairment: Parties whose legally protected interests may be impaired by the litigation must be joined.
c) Multiple Liability Risk: Parties whose absence creates risk of multiple or inconsistent obligations for existing parties must be joined.

Feasibility Analysis

Joinder is feasible when:

- The court can obtain personal jurisdiction over absentees
- Joinder will not destroy subject matter jurisdiction
- Venue is proper for claims involving absentees
- Service of process is possible

Indispensable Party Analysis (Rule 19(b))

When required parties cannot be joined, courts must determine whether to proceed without them or dismiss the action entirely. Courts consider:

- Prejudice to existing parties and absentees
- Availability of measures to limit prejudice
- Whether judgment without absentees would be adequate
- Whether plaintiff would have adequate remedy if action is dismissed

Strategic Considerations

1. Early Identification: Attorneys must identify potentially required parties during case planning to avoid later dismissal or complex joinder motions.
2. Jurisdictional Planning: Required party analysis affects forum selection and may require choosing venues where all necessary parties can be joined.

3. Settlement Coordination: Complex cases may require coordinated settlement discussions with all required parties to achieve complete resolution.

Practical Applications

1. Insurance Coverage: Coverage disputes often involve required joinder of insurers, insureds, and claimants to ensure complete resolution.
2. Contract Disputes: Multi-party contracts frequently require joinder of all parties to avoid inconsistent judgments about rights and obligations.
3. Real Property: Property disputes typically require joinder of all parties with interests in the disputed property.

Common Examination Issues

1. Three-Step Analysis: Students must methodically apply the required party test, feasibility analysis, and indispensable party determination.
2. Jurisdiction Impact: Understanding how required party joinder affects subject matter jurisdiction in diversity and supplemental jurisdiction contexts.

RULE 20. PERMISSIVE JOINDER OF PARTIES

"(a) Persons Who May Join or Be Joined. (1) Plaintiffs. Persons may join in one action as plaintiffs if: (A) they assert any right to relief jointly, severally, or in the alternative with respect to or arising out of the same transaction, occurrence, or series of transactions or occurrences; and (B) any question of law or fact common to all plaintiffs will arise in the action."

Core Requirements

Rule 20 allows, but does not require, joinder of multiple plaintiffs or defendants when efficiency benefits outweigh complexity costs. The rule requires both transactional relationship and common questions.

Two-Prong Test:

a) Same Transaction or Occurrence: Claims must arise from the same transaction, occurrence, or series of related transactions or occurrences
b) Common Questions: At least one question of law or fact must be common to all joined parties

Liberal Interpretation: Courts interpret these requirements broadly to promote judicial efficiency and consistent outcomes.

Plaintiff Joinder (Rule 20(a)(1))

Multiple plaintiffs may join when they have related claims against defendants. Common scenarios include:

- Product liability cases with multiple injured consumers
- Securities fraud affecting multiple investors
- Environmental contamination harming multiple property owners

- Employment discrimination affecting multiple workers

Defendant Joinder (Rule 20(a)(2))

Multiple defendants may be joined when plaintiffs have related claims against them:

- Joint tortfeasors in accident cases
- Co-conspirators in antitrust violations
- Multiple contractors in construction disputes
- Chain of distribution in product liability cases

Jurisdictional Requirements

1. Subject Matter Jurisdiction: Each claim must satisfy federal jurisdiction requirements or qualify for supplemental jurisdiction.
2. Personal Jurisdiction: The court must have personal jurisdiction over each joined party, though different jurisdictional bases may support different parties.
3. Venue: Venue must be proper for the action as a whole, typically satisfied if proper as to any defendant under 28 U.S.C. § 1391.

Severance and Separate Trials (Rule 20(b))

Courts have broad discretion to order separate trials or sever improperly joined parties to:

- Avoid prejudice or confusion

- Expedite resolution
- Reduce costs
- Ensure fair adjudication

Strategic Applications

1. Cost Efficiency: Permissive joinder reduces duplicative discovery, expert witnesses, and trial preparation costs.
2. Settlement Dynamics: Multiple parties can create complex settlement negotiations but may provide additional leverage.
3. Trial Strategy: Joined parties may present consistent theories or create conflicts that benefit or harm case presentation.

Common Examination Issues

1. Transaction Analysis: Students must determine whether factually related events constitute the "same transaction or occurrence" under Rule 20.
2. Supplemental Jurisdiction: Understanding how permissive joinder interacts with supplemental jurisdiction requirements in diversity cases.
3. Strategic Evaluation: Analyzing whether permissive joinder is advisable given case complexity and management considerations.

RULE 21. MISJOINDER AND NONJOINDER OF PARTIES

"Misjoinder of parties is not a ground for dismissing an action. On motion or on its own, the court may at any time, on just terms, add or drop parties. The court may also sever any claim against a party."

Core Requirements

Rule 21 provides courts with flexible authority to correct party problems without dismissing meritorious actions. The rule prioritizes substance over procedural technicalities.

Misjoinder Correction: When parties are improperly joined under Rules 19 or 20, courts can drop parties rather than dismiss the action.

Nonjoinder Correction: When required parties are absent, courts can order joinder of additional parties if feasible.

Severance Authority: Courts can separate improperly joined claims or parties into separate actions for efficient case management.

Judicial Discretion

Courts exercise broad discretion in applying Rule 21, considering:

- Fairness to all parties
- Judicial efficiency

- Costs and complexity
- Stage of litigation when motion is made

Practical Applications

1. Case Salvage: Rule 21 prevents dismissal of otherwise meritorious actions due to party joinder errors.
2. Discovery Management: Severance can prevent discovery disputes from affecting unrelated claims or parties.
3. Trial Efficiency: Separating complex multi-party cases can simplify trial presentation and jury comprehension.

Strategic Considerations

1. Early Motion Practice: Party joinder challenges are often best addressed early in litigation before substantial discovery occurs.
2. Coordination Issues: Severed actions may require coordination to prevent inconsistent judgments and duplicative proceedings.

RULE 22. INTERPLEADER

"(a) Grounds. (1) By a Plaintiff. Persons with claims that may expose a plaintiff to double or multiple liability may be joined as defendants and required to interplead..."

Core Requirements

Interpleader allows parties holding disputed funds or property to force claimants to litigate their competing claims in a single action, protecting stakeholders from multiple liability.

Stakeholder Protection: The primary purpose is protecting parties who hold disputed stakes from multiple lawsuits and inconsistent judgments.

Claimant Requirements: Multiple parties must claim entitlement to the same stake, creating potential multiple liability for the stakeholder.

Dispute Requirement: The stakeholder need not determine which claimant has superior rights but must face genuine competing claims.

Two Types of Interpleader

Rule Interpleader (Rule 22): Uses normal federal jurisdiction requirements

- Requires complete diversity between stakeholder and all claimants
- Amount in controversy must exceed $75,000
- Limited venue options

Statutory Interpleader (28 U.S.C. § 1335): Provides broader federal jurisdiction

- Requires only minimal diversity (any two claimants from different states)

- Amount in controversy only $500
- Nationwide service of process
- More flexible venue provisions

Practical Applications

1. Insurance Proceeds: Life insurance companies use interpleader when multiple beneficiaries claim the same policy proceeds.
2. Escrow Disputes: Real estate closings with title disputes often require interpleader of purchase funds.
3. Employment Benefits: Retirement plan administrators use interpleader when divorce and beneficiary designations conflict.
4. Construction Projects: Contractors may interplead disputed lien funds when multiple subcontractors claim priority.

Procedural Mechanics

1. Stakeholder Deposit: Courts typically require deposit of disputed funds or property into the court registry.
2. Discharge Option: Stakeholders may seek discharge from further liability once interpleader is established and stakes deposited.
3. Claimant Litigation: After stakeholder withdrawal, claimants litigate priority rights among themselves.

Strategic Considerations

1. Early Filing: Stakeholders benefit from filing interpleader before facing multiple lawsuits in different courts.
2. Cost Allocation: Courts may award attorney fees and costs from the disputed stake or allocate them among claimants.
3. Jurisdictional Choice: Comparing Rule 22 and statutory interpleader requirements helps determine optimal federal court access.

Common Examination Issues

1. Jurisdiction Analysis: Students must distinguish between Rule 22 and statutory interpleader jurisdiction requirements.
2. Stakeholder Status: Identifying when parties qualify as proper stakeholders versus interested claimants.
3. Multiple Liability: Understanding what constitutes genuine risk of double or multiple liability sufficient for interpleader.

RULE 23. CLASS ACTIONS

"(a) Prerequisites. One or more members of a class may sue or be sued as representative parties on behalf of all members only if: (1) the class is so numerous that joinder of all members is impracticable; (2) there are questions of law or fact common to the class; (3) the claims or defenses of the representative parties are typical of the claims or defenses of the class; and (4) the representative parties will fairly and adequately protect the interests of the class."

Core Requirements (Rule 23(a) Prerequisites)

All class actions must satisfy four mandatory requirements before courts can consider certification:

Numerosity: The class must be so numerous that individual joinder is impracticable. While no specific number is required, courts typically require:

- Generally 40+ members for presumption of impracticability
- Smaller classes may qualify with geographic dispersion or other joinder barriers
- Very large classes (thousands) easily satisfy numerosity

Commonality: Common questions of law or fact must exist among class members. This requires:

- Shared legal or factual issues across the class
- Questions capable of class-wide resolution
- More than merely identical legal theories (must be common answers)

Typicality: Representative parties' claims must be typical of class claims. This ensures:

- Representatives have same basic legal theory as class members

- No fundamental conflicts between representatives and class
- Similar factual circumstances underlying claims

Adequacy: Representative parties and counsel must fairly and adequately protect class interests:

- Representatives cannot have interests antagonistic to the class
- Counsel must be competent and experienced in class action litigation
- Sufficient resources to prosecute the action effectively

Class Action Categories (Rule 23(b))

Rule 23(b)(1) Classes: Prosecuting separate actions would create risk of:

- Incompatible standards of conduct for the opposing party
- Adjudications that would impair absent class members' interests

Rule 23(b)(2) Classes: Opposing party has acted on grounds generally applicable to the class, making injunctive or declaratory relief appropriate for the class as a whole. Common in:

- Civil rights litigation
- Environmental enforcement
- Employment discrimination cases

Rule 23(b)(3) Classes: Common questions predominate over individual issues and class action is superior to other methods for fair and efficient adjudication. Courts consider:

- Class members' interests in individual control
- Extent and nature of pending litigation
- Desirability of concentrating litigation in one forum
- Difficulties in managing class action

Notice Requirements

Rule 23(b)(3) Notice: Due process requires individual notice to identifiable class members in damages class actions, including:

- Nature of the action
- Definition of certified class
- Class claims and defenses
- Right to opt out and consequences
- Right to appear through counsel
- Binding effect of judgment

Rule 23(b)(1) and (b)(2) Notice: Courts have discretion to order notice but it is not constitutionally required for mandatory classes.

Settlement and Dismissal (Rule 23(e))

Class action settlements require court approval with procedural safeguards:

- Notice to class members
- Fairness hearing
- Court determination that settlement is fair, reasonable, and adequate
- Opportunity for objections

Practical Applications

1. Securities Fraud: Rule 23(b)(3) classes allow investors to pursue damages collectively against corporations and auditors.
2. Product Liability: Defective product cases often proceed as class actions when individual claims are too small for separate litigation.
3. Consumer Protection: Deceptive practice cases frequently use class treatment when individual damages are modest but aggregate harm is substantial.
4. Civil Rights: Institutional reform litigation typically proceeds under Rule 23(b)(2) seeking systemic injunctive relief.

Strategic Considerations

1. Certification Strategy: Plaintiffs must carefully craft class definitions and choose representatives to maximize certification chances.
2. Discovery Focus: Early discovery should focus on class certification requirements rather than merits to resolve certification promptly.

3. Settlement Timing: Class certification status significantly affects settlement value and negotiation dynamics.
4. Opt-Out Considerations: In Rule 23(b)(3) classes, significant opt-outs can undermine class viability and settlement value.

Common Certification Challenges

1. Predominance Analysis: Showing that common issues predominate over individual issues in Rule 23(b)(3) classes.
2. Manageability: Demonstrating that class treatment is superior to individual litigation or other resolution methods.
3. Damages Calculation: Establishing that damages can be calculated on class-wide basis without excessive individual inquiries.

Common Examination Issues

1. Certification Requirements: Students must systematically apply Rule 23(a) and (b) requirements to proposed class definitions.
2. Notice Analysis: Understanding different notice requirements for different types of class actions.
3. Settlement Approval: Analyzing whether proposed class settlements meet fairness and adequacy standards.

RULE 23.1. DERIVATIVE ACTIONS

"(a) Prerequisites. This rule applies when one or more shareholders or members of a corporation or an unincorporated association bring a derivative action to enforce a right that the corporation or association may properly assert but has failed to enforce..."

Core Requirements

Derivative actions allow shareholders and members to sue on behalf of corporations or associations when management fails to pursue valid claims. The rule ensures legitimate representative litigation while preventing abusive suits.

Standing Requirements:

- Plaintiff must have been a shareholder/member when the alleged wrongdoing occurred
- Plaintiff must remain a shareholder/member throughout litigation
- Plaintiff must fairly and adequately represent corporate/association interests

Demand Requirement (Rule 23.1(b)): Before filing suit, plaintiff must generally make demand on the corporation's board of directors (or association's management) to pursue the claim, unless demand would be futile.

Complaint Allegations: The derivative complaint must allege:

- Plaintiff's shareholder/member status at relevant times

- That demand was made or reasons why demand is futile
- That the action is not collusive

Demand Futility Analysis

Courts excuse demand requirements when:

- Board members are personally interested in the challenged transaction
- Board lacks independence due to control relationships
- Challenged conduct cannot be ratified under applicable law
- Demand would be meaningless due to management hostility

Settlement and Dismissal (Rule 23.1(c))

Derivative actions cannot be dismissed or settled without court approval and notice to shareholders/members because:

- Management that refused initial demand cannot later settle away corporate rights
- Court oversight prevents collusive settlements that benefit plaintiffs' attorneys at corporate expense
- Shareholder/member notice allows objections to inadequate settlements

Practical Applications

1. Executive Compensation: Shareholders challenge excessive executive compensation through derivative suits when boards approve unreasonable packages.
2. Self-Dealing Transactions: Derivative suits address transactions where directors or officers benefit personally at corporate expense.
3. Corporate Waste: Shareholders can challenge management decisions that waste corporate assets or opportunities.
4. Breach of Fiduciary Duty: Directors and officers who breach duties to the corporation face derivative liability.

Strategic Considerations

1. Demand Decisions: Whether to make demand or claim futility affects litigation strategy and timing significantly.
2. Settlement Value: Derivative settlements must benefit the corporation rather than individual shareholders, affecting valuation methods.
3. Attorney Fees: Successful derivative plaintiffs can recover attorney fees from the corporation under the common fund doctrine.

State Law Integration

1. Substantive Standards: State corporate law governs substantive claims in derivative actions, while Rule 23.1 provides procedural framework.
2. Demand Requirements: State law may impose additional or different demand requirements that affect federal derivative actions.

Common Examination Issues

1. Demand Analysis: Students must determine whether demand is required and whether circumstances excuse the demand requirement.
2. Settlement Approval: Understanding court supervision requirements for derivative settlement approval.
3. Standing Requirements: Analyzing whether plaintiffs meet continuous shareholder/member status requirements.

RULE 23.2. ACTIONS RELATING TO UNINCORPORATED ASSOCIATIONS

"This rule applies to an action brought by or against the members of an unincorporated association as a class by naming certain members as representative parties..."

Core Requirements

Rule 23.2 provides a streamlined procedure for suing unincorporated associations without requiring joinder of all members or formal class action certification under Rule 23.

Association Definition: Unincorporated associations include:

- Labor unions
- Professional associations
- Trade associations
- Social clubs
- Religious organizations
- Partnerships in some contexts

Representative Suit Authority: Members can sue or be sued as representatives of the association without satisfying all Rule 23 class action requirements, provided:

- Representatives adequately represent association interests
- The action relates to association affairs or common member interests
- Individual member rights are not prejudiced

Practical Applications

1. Labor Disputes: Union members can challenge association decisions or sue on behalf of the union without complex class certification procedures.

2. Professional Associations: Members can seek injunctive relief regarding association governance or challenge disciplinary actions.
3. Trade Association Disputes: Business association members can resolve disputes about association policies or actions.

Strategic Advantages

1. Simplified Procedure: Avoids complex class certification requirements while providing representative suit benefits.
2. Efficiency: Allows resolution of association-wide disputes without joining hundreds or thousands of individual members.
3. Flexibility: Courts can tailor procedures to fit specific association structures and dispute types.

Common Examination Issues

1. Association Identification: Students must distinguish between incorporated entities (subject to normal party rules) and unincorporated associations eligible for Rule 23.2 treatment.
2. Adequacy Analysis: Understanding how courts evaluate representative adequacy without full Rule 23 class action safeguards.

RULE 24. INTERVENTION

"(a) Intervention of Right. On timely motion, the court must permit anyone to intervene who: (1) is given an unconditional right to intervene by a federal statute; or (2) claims an interest relating to the property or transaction that is the subject of the action, and is so situated that disposing of the action may as a practical matter impair or impede the movant's ability to protect that interest, unless existing parties adequately represent that interest."

Core Requirements

Intervention allows non-parties to join ongoing litigation either as a matter of right or with court permission. The rule balances efficiency against the rights of interested parties to protect their interests.

Intervention of Right (Rule 24(a))

Statutory Right: Federal statutes may grant unconditional intervention rights in specific circumstances.

Interest-Based Right: Courts must allow intervention when:

- Movant has a legally protectable interest in the action's subject matter
- Disposition may impair movant's ability to protect that interest
- Existing parties do not adequately represent movant's interests

- Motion is timely filed

Permissive Intervention (Rule 24(b))

Courts may permit intervention when:

- Federal statute grants conditional intervention right
- Movant's claim or defense shares common questions of law or fact with the main action
- Intervention will not unduly delay or prejudice existing parties

Timeliness Analysis

Courts consider multiple factors for timeliness:

- Length of time between knowledge of interest and motion to intervene
- Reason for delay
- Prejudice to existing parties from intervention
- Prejudice to movant if intervention is denied

Interest Requirements

Protectable Interest: Movants must demonstrate legally recognized interests, not merely economic concerns or general policy preferences:

- Property rights in disputed assets
- Contractual rights affected by litigation outcome

- Regulatory interests for government agencies
- Beneficiary rights in trust or insurance disputes

Impairment Analysis: Potential impairment must be practical and direct, not speculative or remote.

Inadequate Representation: Movants must show existing parties do not adequately represent their interests due to different priorities, conflicts, or insufficient advocacy.

Practical Applications

1. Insurance Coverage: Additional insurers intervene in coverage disputes affecting multiple policies or layers of coverage.
2. Government Actions: Regulatory agencies intervene in private litigation affecting public interests they are charged to protect.
3. Contract Disputes: Third-party beneficiaries intervene in contract litigation affecting their rights.
4. Environmental Cases: Environmental groups intervene in government enforcement actions seeking stronger remedies.

Strategic Considerations

1. Timing Strategy: Early intervention provides maximum litigation participation rights, while late intervention may be limited to specific issues.

2. Representation Analysis: Potential intervenors must evaluate whether existing parties will adequately protect their interests or present conflicting priorities.
3. Case Complexity: Courts balance intervention benefits against increased complexity and potential delay.

Common Examination Issues

1. Interest Analysis: Students must identify what constitutes sufficient legal interest for intervention of right.
2. Timeliness Factors: Understanding how courts balance various timeliness considerations in intervention analysis.
3. Adequate Representation: Analyzing whether existing parties provide sufficient representation to defeat intervention motions.

RULE 25. SUBSTITUTION OF PARTIES

"(a) Death. (1) Substitution if the Claim Is Not Extinguished. If a party dies and the claim is not extinguished, the court may order substitution of the proper party..."

Core Requirements

Rule 25 addresses what happens when parties die, become incapacitated, or transfer their interests during litigation. The rule ensures that litigation can continue despite changes in party status.

Death of Parties (Rule 25(a))

When parties die during litigation:

- Courts may substitute proper representatives if claims survive the party's death
- Substitution motion must be made within 90 days after death is suggested on the record
- Failure to substitute timely results in action dismissal as to deceased party
- Claims that do not survive death are dismissed rather than substituted

Incompetency (Rule 25(b))

When parties become incompetent:

- Courts may substitute guardians, conservators, or other representatives
- Existing representation may continue if it adequately protects the incompetent party's interests
- Courts have discretion to require formal substitution or allow informal continuation

Transfer of Interest (Rule 25(c))

When parties transfer their interests:

- Original parties may continue litigation if they retain sufficient interest
- Transferees may be substituted or joined as additional parties
- Courts consider whether transfer was made to evade litigation obligations

Public Officer Substitution (Rule 25(d))

When public officers are parties in their official capacity:

- Successor officers are automatically substituted
- No formal substitution motion required
- Litigation continues seamlessly despite personnel changes

Survival of Claims

1. State Law Governs: In diversity cases, state survival statutes determine whether claims survive a party's death and can be prosecuted by representatives.
2. Federal Claims: Federal law governs survival of federal statutory claims, with varying results depending on specific statutes.

Practical Applications

1. Personal Injury Cases: When plaintiffs die during litigation, representatives may continue wrongful death or survival claims under applicable state law.
2. Contract Disputes: Business litigation often continues when key principals die, with corporate succession or estate representatives.
3. Real Estate Litigation: Property disputes frequently require substitution when owners die during lengthy proceedings.

Strategic Considerations

1. Early Planning: Estate planning attorneys should consider potential litigation when drafting wills and establishing representative authority.
2. Settlement Timing: Pending death or incapacity may affect settlement negotiations and authority to resolve claims.
3. Insurance Coordination: Life insurance and liability coverage may be affected by death and substitution timing.

Procedural Mechanics

1. Motion Requirements: Substitution motions must identify proper representatives and demonstrate their authority to continue litigation.

2. Notice Requirements: All parties must receive notice of substitution motions and proposed representatives.
3. Discovery Impact: Substitution may affect discovery scope and witness availability, requiring case management adjustments.

Common Examination Issues

1. 90-Day Rule: Students must understand the strict 90-day deadline for death substitution motions and consequences of missing deadlines.
2. Survival Analysis: Determining whether specific types of claims survive party death under applicable state or federal law.
3. Representative Authority: Analyzing whether proposed substitute parties have legal authority to continue litigation.

INTEGRATION WITH OTHER RULES

Supplemental Jurisdiction Considerations

28 U.S.C. § 1367 Analysis: Party joinder rules frequently interact with supplemental jurisdiction requirements:

1. Related claims typically qualify for supplemental jurisdiction
2. Diversity cases have specific limitations on claims by plaintiffs against non-diverse parties
3. Court discretion to decline supplemental jurisdiction affects joinder strategy

Discovery Coordination

Multi-party litigation creates complex discovery management issues:

- Coordinated discovery reduces duplication and costs
- Conflicting party interests may require separate discovery tracks
- Protective orders become crucial with multiple parties and sensitive information

Settlement Dynamics

Multiple parties create complex settlement considerations:

- Joint defense agreements coordinate strategy among defendants
- Settlement timing affects remaining parties' positions
- Contribution and indemnity rights affect settlement values
- Class action settlements require court approval and member notice

Case Management Challenges

Courts actively manage multi-party cases through:

- Early case management conferences
- Staged discovery and motion practice
- Separate trial tracks for efficiency
- Coordination with related actions in other courts

Strategic Planning Integration

Effective multi-party litigation requires:

- Early identification of all potentially necessary parties
- Jurisdictional planning to ensure all parties can be joined
- Discovery coordination to manage costs and complexity
- Settlement strategy accounting for multiple party dynamics

Common Multi-Party Pitfalls

1. Jurisdiction Destruction: Adding non-diverse parties can destroy diversity jurisdiction without supplemental jurisdiction protection.
2. Venue Problems: Additional parties may create venue complications requiring transfer or dismissal.
3. Service Complications: Multiple parties, especially foreign or hard-to-serve defendants, can create service deadline problems under Rule 4(m).
4. Management Complexity: Poorly planned multi-party litigation can become unmanageable, leading to severance or dismissal.

TITLE V - DISCLOSURES AND DISCOVERY

Title V transforms civil litigation from a trial by surprise into a system of informed advocacy through comprehensive information exchange. These rules balance the competing goals of thorough case preparation against litigation costs and abuse prevention. Modern discovery practice shapes case outcomes more than trial advocacy, making mastery of these provisions essential for effective representation. Understanding discovery timing, scope limitations, and sanction mechanisms determines litigation success in the vast majority of cases that settle before trial.

RULE 26. DUTY TO DISCLOSE; GENERAL PROVISIONS GOVERNING DISCOVERY

"(a)(1) Required Disclosures. Except as exempted by Rule 26(a)(1)(B) or as otherwise stipulated or ordered by the court, a party must, without awaiting a discovery request, make the following disclosures..."

Core Requirements

Rule 26 establishes the foundation for all federal discovery practice through mandatory disclosure obligations, scope limitations, and protective mechanisms. The rule creates a three-tier disclosure system supplemented by traditional discovery tools.

Initial Disclosures (Rule 26(a)(1))

Parties must automatically disclose within 14 days after the Rule 26(f) conference:

a) Witnesses: Names and contact information for individuals likely to have discoverable information that the disclosing party may use to support its claims or defenses.
b) Documents: Copy or description of all documents, electronically stored information, and tangible things in the party's possession that it may use to support its claims or defenses.
c) Damages Computation: Computation of claimed damages and supporting documents.
d) Insurance Agreements: Insurance agreements that may cover all or part of any judgment.

Expert Disclosures (Rule 26(a)(2))

Expert witness information must be disclosed at court-ordered times, typically 90 days before trial:

a) Retained Experts: Complete written report including opinions, bases, qualifications, compensation, and prior testimony.

b) Non-Retained Experts: Summary of facts and opinions for employees or treating physicians who may testify as experts.
c) Rebuttal Experts: Disclosure within 30 days after adverse expert disclosure, limited to contradicting or rebutting earlier expert testimony.

Pretrial Disclosures (Rule 26(a)(3))

At least 30 days before trial, parties must disclose:

- Trial witnesses and their anticipated testimony scope
- Documents and exhibits for trial use
- Deposition designations for trial testimony

Discovery Scope (Rule 26(b)(1))

Parties may obtain discovery regarding any nonprivileged matter relevant to any party's claim or defense and proportional to the case's needs, considering:

- Importance of issues at stake
- Amount in controversy
- Parties' relative access to information
- Parties' resources
- Importance of discovery in resolving issues
- Whether burden or expense outweighs likely benefit

Proportionality Analysis

The 2015 amendments elevated proportionality from a protective order consideration to a fundamental scope limitation. Courts must actively manage discovery to ensure proportional case resolution.

Factor Evaluation:

- Case significance beyond monetary stakes
- Complexity of legal and factual issues
- Information asymmetries between parties
- Available resources for discovery
- Alternative information sources

Privilege Protection (Rule 26(b)(1))

1. Attorney-Client Privilege: Communications between attorneys and clients for legal advice purposes remain protected.
2. Work Product Doctrine: Attorney mental impressions, legal theories, and trial preparation materials receive qualified protection.
3. Other Privileges: Federal common law and applicable state privileges protect confidential relationships and sensitive information.

Electronically Stored Information (ESI)

Rule 26(b)(2)(B) addresses electronic discovery challenges:

- Parties need not produce ESI from sources that are not reasonably accessible
- Courts may order discovery from inaccessible sources for good cause
- Cost-shifting provisions apply to expensive electronic discovery
- Safe harbor protects against sanctions for routine electronic data destruction

Discovery Conference (Rule 26(f))

Parties must confer at least 21 days before the scheduling conference to discuss:

- Claims and defenses nature and basis
- Settlement possibilities
- Initial disclosure arrangements
- Discovery plan including ESI issues
- Privilege protection procedures

Protective Orders (Rule 26(c))

Courts may issue protective orders to prevent discovery abuse:

- Limiting discovery scope or methods
- Designating confidential treatment
- Requiring in-camera review
- Restricting disclosure to qualified persons
- Sealing depositions or documents

Practical Applications

1. Case Planning: Rule 26(f) conferences set discovery tone and create collaborative or adversarial dynamics that affect entire case progression.
2. Cost Management: Proportionality requirements force early case evaluation and strategic discovery planning to control expenses.
3. ESI Management: Electronic discovery protocols established early prevent later disputes and excessive costs.

Strategic Considerations

1. Disclosure Strategy: Initial disclosures reveal case theories early, requiring careful consideration of what information to disclose and how to characterize it.
2. Expert Planning: Expert disclosure deadlines require early identification and retention of qualified experts with adequate preparation time.
3. Privilege Logs: Comprehensive privilege logs prevent waiver while providing opposing parties with sufficient information to challenge questionable claims.

Common Examination Issues

1. Proportionality Analysis: Students must balance discovery benefits against costs and burdens using the Rule 26(b)(1) factors.

2. Privilege vs. Work Product: Distinguishing between attorney-client privilege and work product doctrine protection levels and waiver consequences.
3. ESI Issues: Understanding electronic discovery obligations and the interplay between accessibility, cost, and production requirements.

RULE 27. DEPOSITIONS TO PERPETUATE TESTIMONY

"(a) Before an Action Is Filed. (1) Petition. A person who wants to perpetuate testimony may file a verified petition in the district court for the district where any expected adverse party resides..."

Core Requirements

Rule 27 allows preservation of testimony before litigation begins or while appeals are pending. This preventive discovery tool protects against witness unavailability and memory deterioration.

Before Action Filed (Rule 27(a))

Requirements for pre-litigation depositions:

- Verified petition identifying expected parties and witness
- Statement of subject matter and reasons for perpetuation

- Court order authorizing deposition after notice to expected adverse parties
- 20-day notice period unless court shortens time for cause

Pending Appeal (Rule 27(b))

During appeals, parties may perpetuate testimony if:

- Motion demonstrates need to preserve testimony
- Court finds perpetuation necessary to avoid failure or delay of justice
- Notice provided to all parties

Practical Applications

1. Elderly Witnesses: Depositions preserve testimony of aging witnesses whose availability for trial is uncertain.
2. International Witnesses: Foreign witnesses may be deposed before litigation when trial attendance is impractical.
3. Declining Health: Medical conditions that may prevent future testimony justify perpetuation depositions.
4. Business Records: Key employees leaving companies or retiring may have their knowledge preserved through Rule 27 depositions.

Limitations and Requirements

1. Subject Matter Limits: Depositions must relate to reasonably anticipated litigation, not general information gathering.
2. Notice Requirements: Expected adverse parties must receive adequate notice and opportunity to participate.
3. Court Supervision: Courts maintain discretion over whether perpetuation is necessary and appropriate.

Strategic Considerations

1. Insurance Investigations: Insurance companies frequently use Rule 27 depositions to investigate potential claims before formal litigation.
2. Accident Reconstruction: Immediately after accidents, witness depositions may preserve crucial testimony before memories fade.
3. Corporate Transitions: Business reorganizations or acquisitions may require preservation of institutional knowledge through depositions.

Common Examination Issues

1. Timing Requirements: Students must understand the different requirements for pre-litigation versus pending appeal perpetuation depositions.
2. Necessity Standards: Analyzing when courts will find perpetuation "necessary" to prevent testimony loss.

RULE 28. PERSONS BEFORE WHOM DEPOSITIONS MAY BE TAKEN

"(a) Within the United States. (1) In General. Within the United States or a territory or insular possession subject to United States jurisdiction, a deposition must be taken before: (A) an officer authorized to administer oaths either by federal law or by the law in the place of examination..."

Core Requirements

Rule 28 specifies who may preside over depositions and administer oaths to ensure testimony reliability and legal sufficiency.

Domestic Depositions (Rule 28(a))

Authorized Officers:

- Federal court clerks and deputy clerks
- State court judges and clerks
- Notaries public authorized in the jurisdiction
- Other officers authorized to administer oaths under federal or state law

Disqualification: Officers related to parties or attorneys, or financially interested in the action, cannot preside over depositions.

Foreign Depositions (Rule 28(b))

International depositions may be taken before:

- United States consular officers
- Persons appointed by commission or letters rogatory
- Officers authorized by foreign country law to administer oaths
- Any person appointed by agreement of parties

Practical Applications

1. Routine Depositions: Most domestic depositions use notaries public or court reporters authorized to administer oaths.
2. International Discovery: Foreign depositions require coordination with consular services or foreign legal systems.
3. Remote Depositions: Video conference depositions raise questions about officer jurisdiction and oath administration.

Strategic Considerations

1. Cost Management: Officer selection affects deposition costs, with court reporters typically providing combined services.
2. International Coordination: Foreign depositions may require advance diplomatic coordination or treaty compliance.

RULE 29. STIPULATIONS ABOUT DISCOVERY PROCEDURE

"Unless the court orders otherwise, the parties may stipulate that: (a) a deposition may be taken before any person, at any time or place, on any notice, and in the manner specified—in which event it may be used in the same way as any other deposition; and (b) other discovery may be modified..."

Core Requirements

Rule 29 encourages party cooperation by allowing discovery procedure modifications through stipulation, subject to court oversight for fairness.

Permitted Modifications

1. Deposition Procedures: Parties may modify timing, location, notice periods, and presiding officers through agreement.
2. Discovery Methods: Traditional discovery tool requirements can be altered by stipulation.
3. Timing and Deadlines: Discovery schedules may be adjusted cooperatively.

Court Override Authority

Courts may reject stipulations that:

- Prejudice non-stipulating parties

- Interfere with case management
- Abuse the discovery process
- Violate protective orders

Practical Applications

1. Expedited Discovery: Parties may agree to shortened notice periods for urgent depositions.
2. Cost-Sharing: Complex cases often involve stipulated cost-sharing arrangements for expensive discovery.
3. Remote Procedures: Agreements for video depositions or electronic document production streamline modern discovery.

Strategic Considerations

1. Cooperative Advantage: Discovery stipulations can reduce costs and expedite case resolution while maintaining adversarial effectiveness.
2. Precedent Concerns: Stipulations in one case may create expectations for similar arrangements in future litigation.

RULE 30. DEPOSITIONS BY ORAL EXAMINATION

"(a) When a Deposition May Be Taken. A party may, by oral examination, depose any person, including a party, without leave of court except as provided in Rule 30(a)(2)..."

Core Requirements

Rule 30 governs the most common discovery tool, establishing procedures for oral depositions that balance information gathering with witness protection and cost control.

Authorization and Notice

Leave of Court: Generally not required, except for:

- More than 10 depositions per side
- Deposing the same person twice
- Deposing before Rule 26(f) conference (unless agreed or court ordered)

Notice Requirements (Rule 30(b)):

- Reasonable notice to all parties
- Time, place, and deponent identification
- Method of recording (audio, video, stenographic)
- Document production requests (Rule 30(b)(6) notices)

Corporate Depositions (Rule 30(b)(6))

Organizations must designate knowledgeable persons to testify about specified topics:

- Notice must describe matters for examination with reasonable particularity
- Organization must designate one or more persons to testify

- Designated persons must provide organization's knowledge, not personal knowledge
- Preparation duty requires organization to educate designated persons about requested topics

Examination Conduct (Rule 30(c))

1. Examination and Cross-Examination: Any party may examine the deponent, with the party taking the deposition going first.
2. Time Limits: Depositions are limited to one day of seven hours unless court order or stipulation provides otherwise.
3. Objections: Only objections necessary to preserve privilege or enforce court-ordered limitations should be stated concisely.

Recording Methods (Rule 30(b)(3))

1. Stenographic: Traditional court reporter transcription remains the most common method.
2. Audio/Video: Electronic recording may be used with proper notice and equipment standards.
3. Multiple Methods: Parties may record by multiple methods simultaneously.

Protective Measures

Courts may limit deposition scope, duration, or methods to prevent:

- Harassment or embarrassment
- Privileged information disclosure
- Disproportionate burden or expense
- Discovery abuse or bad faith conduct

Practical Applications

1. Fact Witness Discovery: Rule 30 depositions gather testimony from witnesses with relevant knowledge about case facts.
2. Expert Witness Depositions: Opposing experts may be deposed after expert disclosures to challenge opinions and methodology.
3. Party Depositions: Adverse parties may be deposed to obtain admissions and explore case weaknesses.
4. Preservation for Trial: Depositions preserve testimony for trial use when witnesses become unavailable.

Strategic Considerations

1. Preparation Intensity: Deposition preparation often determines examination effectiveness, requiring thorough document review and question planning.

2. Settlement Impact: Deposition testimony frequently drives settlement discussions by revealing case strengths and weaknesses.
3. Trial Strategy: Deposition transcripts become trial exhibits and impeachment tools, requiring consideration of trial use during examination.

Common Examination Issues

1. Rule 30(b)(6) Notices: Students must understand corporate deposition requirements and organization preparation duties.
2. Time and Scope Limits: Analyzing when seven-hour and one-day limitations apply and when extensions are appropriate.
3. Objection Standards: Understanding when objections are proper and how they affect testimony preservation.

RULE 31. DEPOSITIONS BY WRITTEN QUESTIONS

"(a) When a Deposition May Be Taken. (1) Without Leave. A party may, by written questions, depose any person, including a party, without leave of court except as provided in Rule 31(a)(2)..."

Core Requirements

Rule 31 provides a cost-effective alternative to oral depositions for routine testimony, particularly useful for distant witnesses and simple factual inquiries.

Procedure and Notice

1. Question Service: The deposing party serves written questions on all parties, who may serve cross-questions within 14 days.
2. Officer Appointment: A deposition officer reads questions to the deponent and records answers verbatim.
3. Document Production: Written question depositions may include document requests under Rule 34 procedures.

Practical Applications

1. Routine Records: Bank records custodians and similar routine witnesses often testify through written questions.
2. Geographic Efficiency: Distant witnesses may be deposed by written questions to avoid travel costs.
3. Simple Factual Issues: Straightforward factual questions work well in written format when follow-up is unnecessary.

Limitations

1. Flexibility Loss: No ability to follow up on unexpected answers or pursue new lines of inquiry.
2. Credibility Assessment: Written format prevents evaluation of witness demeanor and credibility indicators.
3. Complex Issues: Sophisticated legal or technical issues require oral examination flexibility.

Strategic Considerations

1. Cost-Benefit Analysis: Written depositions reduce travel and attorney time costs but sacrifice examination flexibility.
2. Settlement Impact: Limited information gathering may provide insufficient case evaluation material for settlement discussions.

RULE 32. USING DEPOSITIONS IN COURT PROCEEDINGS

"(a) Using Depositions. (1) In General. At a hearing or trial, all or part of a deposition may be used against a party on these conditions..."

Core Requirements

Rule 32 governs when deposition testimony may be presented at trial, balancing the preference for live testimony against practical necessity and fairness considerations.

Permissible Uses

1. Against Any Party: Deposition testimony may be used against any party who was present or represented at the deposition.
2. Impeachment: Any party's deposition may be used to impeach their trial testimony regardless of availability.
3. Admissions: Party admissions in depositions are admissible as admissions by party opponents.

Unavailability Requirements (Rule 32(a)(4))

Deposition testimony may substitute for trial testimony when witnesses are:

1. Dead or located more than 100 miles from trial
2. Unable to attend due to age, illness, infirmity, or imprisonment
3. Absent despite subpoena service
4. Exceptional circumstances make attendance unreasonable

Practical Applications

1. Impeachment Evidence: Deposition transcripts provide powerful impeachment tools when trial testimony differs from deposition answers.
2. Absent Witness Testimony: Key witness unavailability can be addressed through deposition presentation rather than case dismissal.
3. Expert Witness Efficiency: Expert deposition testimony may be more cost-effective than trial appearance in appropriate cases.

Strategic Considerations

1. Trial Presentation: Video depositions often provide more compelling presentations than transcript readings.
2. Hearsay Concerns: Deposition testimony must satisfy hearsay rules independently of Rule 32 admissibility standards.
3. Cross-Examination Rights: Adequate cross-examination opportunity at deposition affects trial admissibility.

Common Examination Issues

1. Unavailability Standards: Students must analyze whether witness unavailability justifies deposition use instead of live testimony.

2. Party Admissions: Understanding when deposition statements qualify as party admissions versus requiring unavailability.

RULE 33. INTERROGATORIES TO PARTIES

"(a) In General. (1) Number. Unless otherwise stipulated or ordered by the court, a party may serve on any other party no more than 25 written interrogatories, including all discrete subparts..."

Core Requirements

Rule 33 provides a cost-effective method for obtaining factual information and party positions through written questions that must be answered under oath.

Scope and Limitations

1. 25-Question Limit: Each party may serve no more than 25 interrogatories on any other party, including subparts, unless stipulated or court-ordered otherwise.
2. Party Limitation: Interrogatories may only be served on parties, not third-party witnesses.
3. Written Response: Responses must be written, sworn, and served within 30 days of service.

Response Requirements (Rule 33(b))

1. Oath Requirement: Responses must be made under oath by the party or authorized agent.
2. Completeness Duty: Parties must respond fully based on information reasonably available to them.
3. Business Records Option: When answers can be derived from business records, parties may produce records instead of summarizing information.

Objection Standards (Rule 33(b)(4))

1. Proper Objections: Privilege, relevance, proportionality, and other legitimate discovery objections.
2. Waiver Prevention: Specific objection statements prevent waiver of privileges and protections.
3. Partial Responses: Parties must respond to non-objectionable portions while objecting to improper requests.

Practical Applications

1. Factual Foundation: Interrogatories establish basic facts, chronologies, and party positions efficiently.
2. Witness Identification: Standard interrogatories request witness names and contact information for deposition planning.
3. Document Discovery: Interrogatories often precede document requests by identifying potentially relevant document categories.

4. Expert Discovery: Interrogatories may supplement expert disclosure requirements with additional opinion details.

Strategic Considerations

1. Question Crafting: Effective interrogatories require precise drafting to elicit useful information within the 25-question limit.
2. Follow-up Discovery: Interrogatory answers guide subsequent depositions and document requests by identifying promising information sources.
3. Settlement Preparation: Comprehensive interrogatory responses provide settlement negotiation information and reveal case strengths.

Common Pitfalls

1. Subpart Counting: Courts strictly interpret the 25-question limit, counting discrete subparts as separate interrogatories.
2. Evasive Answers: Parties cannot avoid disclosure through technically correct but evasive responses that fail to provide requested information.
3. Timing Coordination: Interrogatory responses often trigger additional discovery deadlines, requiring careful scheduling coordination.

Common Examination Issues

1. 25-Question Analysis: Students must identify whether complex interrogatories exceed the numerical limit through subpart counting.
2. Response Adequacy: Evaluating whether party responses satisfy completeness requirements or constitute evasive non-answers.
3. Business Records Election: Understanding when parties may choose to produce records rather than provide narrative answers.

RULE 34. PRODUCING DOCUMENTS, ELECTRONICALLY STORED INFORMATION, AND TANGIBLE THINGS

"(a) In General. A party may serve on any other party a request (1) to produce and permit the requesting party...to inspect, copy, test, or sample the following items in the responding party's possession, custody, or control: (A) any designated documents or electronically stored information..."

Core Requirements

Rule 34 governs document production, the most voluminous and expensive component of modern discovery. The rule addresses both traditional documents and the complexities of electronic information.

Scope of Production

1. Documents and ESI: All documents, electronically stored information, and tangible things in the responding party's possession, custody, or control.
2. Control Definition: Parties must produce materials they have the practical ability to obtain, even from third parties in some circumstances.
3. Format Specifications: Requesting parties may specify production formats, but responding parties may object and propose alternatives.

ESI-Specific Provisions

Form of Production (Rule 34(b)(2)(E)):

- Documents must be produced as kept in ordinary business or organized by request categories
- ESI may be produced in reasonably usable form
- Parties should meet and confer about ESI format and methods

Metadata Considerations: Production format affects metadata preservation and accessibility for analysis.

Privilege Protection: Inadvertent privilege disclosure receives protection under Rule 26(b)(5) clawback procedures.

Response Requirements (Rule 34(b))

1. 30-Day Response: Parties must respond within 30 days of service with production or objections.
2. Specificity Requirement: Objections must be specific and state grounds with sufficient detail for evaluation.
3. Partial Production: Parties must produce non-objectionable materials while objecting to improper requests.

Inspection Rights

1. On-Site Testing: Parties may request inspection and testing of tangible things at their location.
2. Sampling Authority: Destructive testing requires court approval when it would damage or destroy evidence.
3. Photography/Measurement: Inspection may include photography, measurement, and other non-destructive examination methods.

Practical Applications

1. Email Discovery: Electronic communications often provide the most relevant case evidence and require sophisticated search and review procedures.
2. Financial Records: Accounting documents, bank records, and financial statements support damages calculations and business practice challenges.

3. Technical Documentation: Product liability and intellectual property cases depend heavily on design documents, testing records, and technical specifications
4. Communication Records: Phone records, meeting minutes, and correspondence reveal decision-making processes and party knowledge.

Strategic Considerations

1. ESI Meet and Confer: Early discussion of electronic discovery procedures prevents later disputes and cost overruns.
2. Privilege Review: Document review for privileged materials requires systematic procedures and may justify special master appointment in complex cases.
3. Production Timing: Strategic production timing can affect settlement discussions and motion practice effectiveness.

Cost and Burden Issues

1. Proportionality Analysis: Rule 26(b)(1) proportionality requirements apply to document production scope and methods.
2. Cost-Shifting: Expensive ESI production may justify cost allocation between requesting and producing parties.
3. Sampling Procedures: Large document sets may require statistical sampling or phased production approaches.

Common Examination Issues

1. ESI Format Issues: Students must understand production format options and their implications for metadata and searchability.
2. Possession, Custody, Control: Analyzing whether parties must produce third-party documents over which they exercise control.
3. Proportionality Application: Balancing document production benefits against costs and burdens using Rule 26(b)(1) factors.

RULE 35. PHYSICAL AND MENTAL EXAMINATIONS

"(a) Order for an Examination. (1) In General. The court where the action is pending may order a party whose mental or physical condition...is in controversy to submit to a physical or mental examination by a suitably licensed or certified examiner..."

Core Requirements

Rule 35 provides the only discovery tool requiring court approval, reflecting the invasive nature of compelled medical examinations and the need to balance discovery rights against personal privacy.

Court Order Requirement

1. Good Cause Standard: Moving parties must demonstrate good cause for examination orders beyond mere relevance.
2. In Controversy Requirement: The examined party's physical or mental condition must be genuinely in controversy, not merely related to damages.
3. Qualified Examiner: Court-appointed examiners must have appropriate licensing and qualifications for the examination type.

Good Cause Analysis

Factors courts consider for good cause:

- Specific nature of condition claims
- Adequacy of other available evidence
- Invasiveness of proposed examination
- Examination necessity for case resolution
- Alternative discovery methods

Examination Scope and Conditions

1. Limited Purpose: Examinations must be limited to conditions actually in controversy.
2. Reasonable Conditions: Courts may impose conditions to protect examined parties from harassment or embarrassment.

3. Recording Rights: Parties may request examination recording or observer presence.
4. Multiple Examinations: Additional examinations require separate court orders with renewed good cause showings.

Report Requirements (Rule 35(b))

1. Examiner's Report: Detailed written report including findings, results, diagnoses, and conclusions.
2. Exchange Obligation: Requesting parties must provide copies to examined parties upon request.
3. Reciprocal Disclosure: Examined parties who receive reports must provide copies of their own medical reports about the same condition.
4. Waiver Consequences: Requesting examination reports may waive physician-patient privilege for the same condition.

Practical Applications

1. Personal Injury Cases: Physical injury claims often justify independent medical examinations to evaluate claimed damages.
2. Mental Health Claims: Emotional distress and psychiatric damage claims may require mental health examinations.
3. Disability Disputes: Workers' compensation and disability insurance cases frequently involve compelled medical examinations.

4. Competency Questions: Guardianship and capacity proceedings may require court-ordered psychological evaluations.

Strategic Considerations

1. Timing Strategy: Early examination motions may provide case evaluation tools, while later motions may serve impeachment purposes.
2. Examiner Selection: Qualified neutral examiners provide more credible results than obviously biased experts.
3. Condition Scope: Carefully defining conditions "in controversy" limits examination scope and protects client privacy.

Privacy Protection

1. HIPAA Considerations: Medical examination orders must comply with health information privacy requirements.
2. Sensitive Conditions: Courts provide additional protection for particularly sensitive medical or psychological conditions.
3. Confidentiality Orders: Examination results may be subject to protective orders limiting disclosure.

Common Examination Issues

1. Good Cause Standard: Students must analyze whether specific fact patterns satisfy the heightened good cause requirement.
2. In Controversy Analysis: Understanding when medical conditions are sufficiently central to claims to justify examination orders.
3. Report Exchange: Evaluating strategic implications of requesting examination reports and triggering reciprocal disclosure obligations.

RULE 36. REQUESTS FOR ADMISSION

"(a) Scope and Procedure. (1) Scope. A party may serve on any other party a written request to admit, for purposes of the pending action only, the truth of any matters within the scope of Rule 26(b)(1) relating to: (A) facts, opinions of fact, or the application of law to fact..."

Core Requirements

Rule 36 streamlines trial preparation by establishing undisputed facts and authenticating documents, eliminating the need to prove uncontroversial matters at trial.

Permissible Subjects

1. Factual Matters: Specific facts, opinions of fact, and mixed questions of law and fact.

2. Document Authenticity: Genuineness of documents and other exhibits for trial use.
3. Legal Conclusions: Pure questions of law are generally inappropriate for admission requests.

Response Requirements (Rule 36(a)(4))

1. 30-Day Response: Parties must respond within 30 days of service with admissions, denials, or objections.
2. Good Faith Investigation: Parties must make reasonable inquiry before claiming insufficient knowledge to admit or deny.
3. Specific Denials: Denials must specifically address the requested admission or explain why it cannot be admitted or denied.

Response Options

1. Admit: Unqualified admission establishes the matter conclusively for litigation purposes.
2. Deny: Specific denial puts the matter in issue for trial resolution.
3. Qualified Response: Parties may admit part while denying part of compound requests.
4. Insufficient Knowledge: Parties may claim insufficient knowledge only after reasonable investigation.
5. Object: Privilege, relevance, or other proper objections to inappropriate requests.

Effect of Admissions (Rule 36(b))

1. Conclusive Effect: Admitted matters are conclusively established for the pending action only.
2. Withdrawal Standards: Courts may permit admission withdrawal when it serves justice and when parties relying on admissions won't be prejudiced.
3. Trial Impact: Admitted facts need not be proven at trial, streamlining case presentation.

Cost-Shifting (Rule 36(a)(6))

When parties unreasonably deny requests later proven true at trial:

- Requesting parties may recover reasonable expenses including attorney fees
- Courts consider denial reasonableness and admission importance
- Cost awards encourage good faith evaluation of admission requests

Practical Applications

1. Fact Establishment: Routine background facts, chronologies, and uncontroversial details can be established through admissions rather than trial testimony.

2. Document Authentication: Business records, contracts, and correspondence authenticity can be established without foundation witnesses.
3. Damages Elements: Specific damages calculations or medical expense amounts may be appropriate for admission.
4. Liability Elements: Clear liability facts may be admitted, focusing trial on contested causation or damages issues.

Strategic Considerations

1. Settlement Tool: Admission requests often prompt realistic case evaluation and settlement discussions by highlighting undeniable facts.
2. Trial Preparation: Admissions streamline trial by eliminating the need to prove undisputed matters through testimony.
3. Discovery Coordination: Effective admission requests follow document discovery and depositions that establish factual foundations.

Common Drafting Problems

1. Compound Requests: Complex requests mixing multiple facts allow qualified responses that defeat the purpose.
2. Legal Conclusions: Inappropriate legal conclusion requests generate proper objections rather than useful admissions.
3. Vague Language: Ambiguous requests allow evasive responses based on interpretation disputes.

Common Examination Issues

1. Response Adequacy: Students must evaluate whether denials are sufficiently specific and whether insufficient knowledge claims are justified.
2. Cost-Shifting Analysis: Understanding when unreasonable denials justify expense awards under Rule 36(a)(6).
3. Withdrawal Standards: Analyzing when courts should permit admission withdrawal under Rule 36(b).

RULE 37. FAILURE TO MAKE DISCLOSURES OR TO COOPERATE IN DISCOVERY; SANCTIONS

"(a) Motion for an Order Compelling Disclosure or Discovery...If a party fails to make a disclosure required by Rule 26(a), or if a party fails to respond or responds inadequately to interrogatories, requests for production, or requests for admission under Rule 33, 34, or 36..."

Core Requirements

Rule 37 provides the enforcement mechanism for all discovery obligations through a graduated sanction system designed to ensure compliance while preventing abuse.

Motion to Compel (Rule 37(a))

Prerequisites:

- Meet and confer requirement before filing motion
- Specific description of discovery disputes
- Good faith certification of conference efforts

Available Relief:

- Orders compelling disclosure or discovery responses
- Attorney fee awards against unsuccessful parties
- Designation of facts as established for evasive responses

Failure to Comply with Court Orders (Rule 37(b))

When parties violate discovery orders, courts may impose:

- Facts established against disobedient parties
- Prohibition of evidence supporting claims or defenses
- Striking pleadings in whole or in part
- Staying proceedings until compliance
- Dismissal with or without prejudice
- Default judgment against defendants
- Contempt of court citations

Failure to Disclose (Rule 37(c))

Automatic sanctions for disclosure violations:

- Exclusion of undisclosed evidence at trial

- Additional sanctions including attorney fees
- Harmless error exception prevents exclusion when failure is substantially justified or harmless

Failure to Participate in Rule 26(f) Conference (Rule 37(f))

Courts may require parties who fail to participate in discovery conferences to pay reasonable expenses including attorney fees.

Safe Harbor for ESI (Rule 37(e))

Absent exceptional circumstances, courts cannot impose sanctions for routine electronic information loss resulting from good faith operation of information systems.

Sanction Standards

1. Proportionality: Sanctions must be proportional to the discovery violation and its consequences.
2. Deterrence: Sanctions should deter future discovery abuse while resolving current disputes.
3. Due Process: Serious sanctions require notice and opportunity to be heard before imposition.

Practical Applications

1. Discovery Abuse: Rule 37 motions address discovery stonewalling, evasive responses, and deliberate non-compliance.
2. Case Management: Discovery sanctions maintain court control over case progression and prevent delay tactics.
3. Cost Recovery: Successful Rule 37 motions often include attorney fee awards, shifting discovery costs to non-compliant parties.

Strategic Considerations

1. Meet and Confer: Thorough meet and confer efforts are prerequisite to successful Rule 37 motions and may resolve disputes without court intervention.
2. Sanction Escalation: Courts typically impose progressively severe sanctions for repeated violations, making early compliance crucial.
3. Evidence Exclusion: Rule 37(c) exclusion sanctions can be case-determinative, requiring careful attention to disclosure obligations.

ESI-Specific Issues

1. Litigation Holds: Parties must implement reasonable procedures to preserve relevant electronic information once litigation is reasonably anticipated.
2. Privilege Logs: Inadequate privilege logs may result in privilege waiver or discovery sanctions.

3. Format Disputes: ESI format disagreements may require court resolution through Rule 37 motion practice.

Common Examination Issues

1. Sanction Appropriateness: Students must analyze which Rule 37 sanctions are appropriate for specific discovery violations.
2. Safe Harbor Application: Understanding when routine ESI destruction is protected from sanctions under Rule 37(e).
3. Meet and Confer Requirements: Evaluating whether pre-motion conference efforts satisfy Rule 37 prerequisites.

TITLE VI - TRIALS

Title VI governs the culmination of federal civil litigation, where legal theories and factual disputes receive final resolution through jury trials or bench trials. These rules balance the constitutional right to jury trial with judicial efficiency, establish procedures for presenting evidence and arguments, and provide mechanisms for challenging insufficient evidence before and after verdict. Understanding trial procedures is essential for effective advocacy and case resolution, as trial rules significantly influence settlement negotiations and case preparation strategies.

RULE 38. RIGHT TO A JURY TRIAL; DEMAND

"(a) Right Preserved. The right of trial by jury as declared by the Seventh Amendment to the Constitution—or as provided by a federal statute—is preserved to the parties inviolate."

Core Requirements

Rule 38 preserves the constitutional and statutory right to jury trial while establishing procedural requirements for invoking this fundamental right.

Seventh Amendment Scope

The Seventh Amendment preserves jury trial rights for:

1. Legal claims that existed at common law in 1791
2. Statutory claims that Congress designates for jury trial
3. Legal remedies including monetary damages
4. Actions analogous to common law suits

Equity Exception: Claims seeking equitable relief (injunctions, specific performance, reformation) do not carry jury trial rights under the Seventh Amendment.

Historical Test Application

Courts apply the historical test to determine jury trial rights:

a) Examine the nature of the action and compare it to 18th-century English practice
b) Analyze the remedy sought (legal vs. equitable)
c) Consider statutory provisions for jury trial rights
d) Apply analogical reasoning for modern claims without historical precedent

Demand Requirements (Rule 38(b))

Jury trial demands must be:

- Made in writing
- Served on all parties
- Filed within 14 days after service of the last pleading directed to the issue

Specificity: Demands must specify the issues for which jury trial is requested, or the demand applies to all triable issues.

Waiver Provisions (Rule 38(d))

Jury trial rights are waived by:

- Failure to make timely written demand
- Failure to file demand with the court
- Withdrawal of demand without party consent

Irrevocable Waiver: Once waived, jury trial rights cannot be restored without all parties' consent.

Practical Applications

1. Mixed Cases: When complaints contain both legal and equitable claims, jury trial rights exist for legal issues, with courts typically trying legal claims first.
2. Federal Statutory Claims: Many federal statutes expressly provide jury trial rights even for claims that might not qualify under historical analysis.
3. Removal Cases: Jury trial rights in removed cases depend on federal law analysis, not state court procedures.

Strategic Considerations

1. Demand Timing: Early jury trial demands preserve maximum flexibility while allowing case development to inform trial strategy decisions.
2. Settlement Impact: Jury trial demands often increase settlement values due to unpredictability and higher trial costs.
3. Case Complexity: Complex cases may benefit from bench trials where judges can better manage technical evidence and legal issues.

Common Examination Issues

1. Historical Analysis: Students must apply the Seventh Amendment historical test to determine jury trial availability for various claim types.
2. Demand Timing: Understanding the 14-day deadline and consequences of missing the demand requirement.
3. Mixed Legal/Equitable Cases: Analyzing jury trial rights when complaints contain both types of claims.

RULE 39. TRIAL BY JURY OR BY THE COURT

"(a) When a Demand Is Made. When a jury trial has been demanded under Rule 38, the action must be designated on the docket as a jury action..."

Core Requirements

Rule 39 implements jury trial demands and provides court discretion for cases without proper demands, while establishing procedures for mixed jury and bench trial issues.

Jury Trial Implementation (Rule 39(a))

When proper jury trial demands are made:

- Cases must be designated as jury actions on court dockets
- All triable issues go to the jury unless otherwise specified
- Courts cannot override proper jury trial demands

Court Discretion (Rule 39(b))

When no jury trial demand is made or rights are waived:

- Courts may order jury trials in their discretion
- Parties may consent to jury trials after waiver
- Courts typically honor party preferences for bench trials

Advisory Jury (Rule 39(c))

In cases without jury trial rights, courts may empanel advisory juries to:

- Assist with fact-finding in complex cases

- Provide community input on disputed issues
- Help courts understand evidence presentation effectiveness

Advisory jury verdicts are not binding but provide guidance for judicial decision-making.

Practical Applications

1. Case Management: Jury trial designation affects scheduling, discovery deadlines, and trial preparation requirements.
2. Settlement Dynamics: Jury trial elections significantly influence settlement negotiations and case valuation.
3. Complex Litigation: Courts may use advisory juries in complex equity cases to assist with factual determinations.

Strategic Considerations

1. Waiver Decisions: Strategic waiver of jury trial rights may benefit cases involving complex technical issues or unsympathetic facts.
2. Advisory Jury Value: Even non-binding advisory jury verdicts provide valuable insight into case strengths and weaknesses.

RULE 40. SCHEDULING CASES FOR TRIAL

"Each court must provide by rule for scheduling trials. The court must give priority to actions entitled to priority by a federal statute."

Core Requirements

Rule 40 delegates trial scheduling authority to individual district courts while requiring priority for statutorily designated cases.

Local Rule Authority

District courts establish trial scheduling procedures through local rules addressing:

- Trial calendar management systems
- Notice requirements for trial settings
- Continuance standards and procedures
- Priority case identification and handling

Statutory Priorities

Federal statutes grant trial priority to:

- Criminal cases under the Speedy Trial Act
- Certain civil rights actions
- Social Security disability appeals
- Patent infringement cases

- Other specifically designated matters

Practical Applications

1. Case Planning: Local trial scheduling rules significantly affect litigation timing and strategy development.
2. Continuance Practice: Understanding local continuance standards helps attorneys manage conflicting schedule demands.
3. Priority Cases: Statutory priority cases receive expedited trial settings that affect preparation time and resource allocation.

Strategic Considerations

1. Calendar Management: Effective trial calendar management requires understanding local court practices and judicial preferences.
2. Settlement Timing: Trial setting dates often drive settlement negotiations and resolution timing.

RULE 41. DISMISSAL OF ACTIONS

"(a) Voluntary Dismissal. (1) By the Plaintiff. (A) Without a Court Order. Subject to Rules 23(e), 23.1(c), and 66 and any applicable federal statute, the plaintiff may dismiss an action without a court order by filing: (i) a notice of dismissal before the opposing party serves either an answer or a motion for summary judgment, whichever is first..."

Core Requirements

Rule 41 provides mechanisms for case dismissal before trial, balancing plaintiff autonomy with defendant protection against harassment and abuse.

Voluntary Dismissal Without Court Order (Rule 41(a)(1)(A))

Plaintiffs may dismiss actions without court approval by filing notice of dismissal before defendants serve:

- An answer to the complaint, or
- A motion for summary judgment
- Whichever occurs first

Absolute Right: This dismissal right is absolute and requires no court approval or opposing party consent.

Voluntary Dismissal by Stipulation (Rule 41(a)(1)(B))

After answer or summary judgment motion service, plaintiffs may dismiss actions only by:

- Stipulation signed by all parties who have appeared, or
- Court order under Rule 41(a)(2)

Court-Ordered Voluntary Dismissal (Rule 41(a)(2))

Courts may grant dismissal motions on terms they deem proper, including:

- Cost payments to defendants
- Conditional dismissals with prejudice
- Security for potential refiling costs
- Other protective conditions

Effect of Voluntary Dismissals

1. Without Prejudice: Voluntary dismissals under Rule 41(a)(1) are without prejudice unless the notice states otherwise.
2. Two-Dismissal Rule: A second dismissal of the same claim operates as an adjudication on the merits (with prejudice).
3. Statute of Limitations: Voluntary dismissals do not toll limitation periods, potentially barring refiling.

Involuntary Dismissal (Rule 41(b))

Courts may dismiss actions involuntarily for:

- Failure to prosecute
- Failure to comply with court orders
- Failure to comply with the Federal Rules
- Any other specified reasons

With Prejudice: Involuntary dismissals typically operate as adjudications on the merits unless otherwise specified.

Practical Applications

1. Strategic Dismissals: Plaintiffs use voluntary dismissals to correct pleading defects, address jurisdiction problems, or respond to strong defense motions.
2. Forum Shopping: Voluntary dismissals may facilitate refiling in more favorable forums, subject to limitation period constraints.
3. Settlement Negotiations: Dismissal threats can affect settlement leverage, particularly when refiling faces limitation problems.

Strategic Considerations

1. Timing Awareness: Understanding answer and summary judgment motion filing deadlines is crucial for preserving absolute dismissal rights.
2. Limitation Period Analysis: Voluntary dismissals require careful limitation period analysis to ensure refiling remains possible.
3. Cost-Benefit Evaluation: Court-ordered dismissals may include cost-shifting provisions that affect dismissal economics.

Common Examination Issues

1. Two-Dismissal Rule: Students must identify when second dismissals operate as merits adjudications under Rule 41(a)(1).

2. Timing Analysis: Understanding the critical deadlines that determine whether court approval is required for voluntary dismissal.
3. Prejudice Analysis: Distinguishing between dismissals with and without prejudice and their preclusive effects.

RULE 42. CONSOLIDATION; SEPARATE TRIALS

"(a) Consolidation. If actions before the court involve a common question of law or fact, the court may: (1) join for hearing or trial any or all matters at issue in the actions; (2) consolidate the actions; or (3) issue any other orders concerning proceedings to avoid unnecessary cost or delay."

Core Requirements

Rule 42 provides courts with broad discretion to manage related cases through consolidation or severance, promoting efficiency while protecting party rights.

Consolidation Standards (Rule 42(a))

Courts may consolidate cases involving:

- Common questions of law or fact
- Efficiency benefits outweighing complexity costs
- No substantial prejudice to party rights
- Administrative convenience and judicial economy

Types of Consolidation:

- Complete consolidation merging cases into single action
- Consolidation for pretrial purposes only
- Joint trial with separate verdicts
- Coordinated discovery and motion practice

Separate Trials (Rule 42(b))

Courts may order separate trials for:

- Separate issues within single cases
- Claims or counterclaims requiring different treatment
- Parties whose interests conflict or create prejudice
- Efficiency or convenience considerations

Common Severance Situations:

- Liability and damages phases in complex cases
- Different defendants with conflicting defenses
- Claims requiring different juries or legal standards
- Prejudicial evidence affecting only some issues

Practical Applications

1. Mass Tort Litigation: Related personal injury cases often benefit from consolidated discovery with separate trials on individual damages.
2. Commercial Disputes: Business cases involving common contract interpretation may be consolidated while preserving individual damage calculations.

3. Class Actions: Courts frequently bifurcate class certification from merits determinations to manage case complexity.

Strategic Considerations

1. Efficiency vs. Complexity: Parties must balance consolidation efficiency benefits against increased case complexity and potential confusion.
2. Prejudice Analysis: Consolidation opponents must demonstrate specific prejudice rather than general inconvenience.
3. Settlement Impact: Consolidation significantly affects settlement dynamics by changing party leverage and coordination requirements.

Common Examination Issues

1. Common Question Analysis: Students must identify sufficient legal or factual commonality to justify consolidation under Rule 42(a).
2. Prejudice Evaluation: Understanding when consolidation creates unfair prejudice requiring separate trials.
3. Judicial Discretion: Analyzing the broad discretion courts possess in making consolidation and severance decisions.

RULE 43. TAKING TESTIMONY

"(a) In General. At trial, the witnesses' testimony must be taken orally in open court unless a federal statute, the Federal Rules of Evidence, these rules, or other rules adopted by the Supreme Court provide otherwise..."

Core Requirements

Rule 43 establishes live testimony as the preferred method for trial evidence while providing exceptions for alternative presentation methods.

Oral Testimony Requirement (Rule 43(a))

1. General Rule: Trial testimony must be given orally in open court with witnesses physically present.
2. Oath Requirement: All witnesses must testify under oath or affirmation administered by authorized court officers.
3. Cross-Examination Rights: Parties have fundamental rights to cross-examine adverse witnesses.

Alternative Testimony Methods (Rule 43(a))

1. Deposition Testimony: Rule 32 governs when depositions may substitute for live testimony.
2. Video Testimony: Courts may permit video conference testimony for witnesses whose attendance is impracticable.

3. Affidavit Evidence: Limited circumstances allow affidavit testimony as provided by Federal Rules of Evidence.

Interpreter Services (Rule 43(d))

Courts must provide qualified interpreters for:

- Non-English speaking witnesses and parties
- Hearing-impaired participants
- Other communication disabilities

Interpreter Oath: Court interpreters must take oaths to provide accurate translation services.

Practical Applications

1. Remote Testimony: Modern technology enables video testimony for distant or unavailable witnesses, subject to court approval and technical standards.
2. Expert Witness Efficiency: Complex expert testimony may benefit from video presentation when physical presence is impracticable.
3. International Witnesses: Foreign witnesses may testify by video conference when visa or travel issues prevent physical attendance.

Strategic Considerations

1. Credibility Assessment: Live testimony allows juries to observe witness demeanor, while remote testimony may diminish credibility evaluation.
2. Technical Reliability: Video testimony requires reliable technology and backup procedures to prevent trial disruptions.
3. Cost Management: Remote testimony can reduce witness travel costs while maintaining effective examination opportunities.

RULE 44. PROVING AN OFFICIAL RECORD

"(a) Means of Proving. (1) Domestic Record. Each of the following evidences an official record—or an entry in it—that is otherwise admissible and is kept within the United States..."

Core Requirements

Rule 44 establishes authentication procedures for official records, creating presumptions of authenticity that streamline trial evidence presentation.

Domestic Records (Rule 44(a)(1))

Official records may be proved by:

- Certified copies with official seals
- Copies attested by authorized custodians

- Copies authenticated under Federal Rules of Evidence
- Other methods authorized by federal statute or rule

Self-Authentication: Properly certified official records are self-authenticating and require no additional foundation evidence.

Foreign Records (Rule 44(a)(2))

Foreign official records require authentication by:

- Final certification from authorized foreign officials
- Diplomatic or consular certification
- Other methods satisfying Federal Rules of Evidence requirements
- Treaty-based authentication procedures

Summary Evidence (Rule 44(b))

When records are voluminous, parties may present:

- Summaries prepared from official records
- Charts and calculations based on official records
- Other condensed presentations, subject to opposing party examination of underlying records

Practical Applications

1. Business Records: Corporate filings, licenses, and regulatory records often qualify for Rule 44 treatment as official records.
2. Real Estate Transactions: Property deeds, mortgages, and title records receive presumptive authenticity under Rule 44 procedures.
3. International Documentation: Foreign government certificates and official documents require careful authentication planning.

Strategic Considerations

1. Foundation Efficiency: Rule 44 procedures eliminate the need for custodial witnesses to authenticate routine official records.
2. International Coordination: Foreign record authentication may require advance diplomatic coordination and treaty compliance.

RULE 44.1. DETERMINING FOREIGN LAW

"A party who intends to raise an issue about a foreign country's law must give notice by a pleading or other writing. In determining foreign law, the court may consider any relevant material or source..."

Core Requirements

Rule 44.1 treats foreign law as a question of law for court determination rather than a fact question for jury consideration.

Notice Requirements

Parties raising foreign law issues must provide:

- Written notice in pleadings or other documents
- Reasonable notice timing to allow opposing party preparation
- Sufficient detail to identify the foreign law issues involved

Court Determination Process

1. Judicial Notice: Courts may take judicial notice of foreign law without party proof.
2. Research Authority: Courts may conduct independent research into foreign law questions.
3. Expert Evidence: Courts may consider expert testimony about foreign law content and interpretation.
4. Scholarly Sources: Legal treatises, court decisions, and academic materials may inform foreign law determinations.

Appellate Review

Foreign law determinations receive de novo appellate review as questions of law rather than clearly erroneous factual review.

Practical Applications

1. International Contracts: Commercial agreements governed by foreign law require Rule 44.1 notice and proof procedures.
2. Immigration Cases: Immigration status determinations often depend on foreign marriage, adoption, or citizenship law.
3. International Torts: Cross-border accidents and injuries may require foreign tort law application and proof.

Strategic Considerations

1. Early Notice: Timely foreign law notice allows adequate preparation time for complex international legal research.
2. Expert Selection: Qualified foreign law experts require careful vetting of credentials and familiarity with relevant legal systems.

RULE 45. SUBPOENA

"(a) In General. (1) Form and Contents. Every subpoena must: (A) state the name of the court from which it is issued; and (B) state the title of the action and its civil-action number..."

Core Requirements

Rule 45 provides broad authority to compel witness attendance and document production from non-parties, subject to geographic limitations and burden protections.

Subpoena Types

1. Trial Subpoenas: Compel witness attendance at trial or hearing.
2. Deposition Subpoenas: Require witness appearance at depositions.
3. Document Subpoenas: Compel document production without witness attendance (subpoena duces tecum).
4. Combined Subpoenas: Require both witness attendance and document production.

Geographic Limitations (Rule 45(c))

Trial Subpoenas: Witnesses can be required to attend trial if they:

- Reside within 100 miles of trial location, or
- Regularly conduct business within the district

- Are served within the state and within 100 miles of trial location

Deposition Subpoenas: More flexible geographic scope allowing service anywhere within the United States for depositions in convenient locations.

Service Requirements (Rule 45(b))

1. Personal Service: Subpoenas must be personally served on witnesses by authorized process servers.
2. Witness Fees: Service must include payment of reasonable witness fees and mileage costs.
3. Notice to Parties: Serving parties must provide copies to all other parties before or promptly after service.

Protection Against Undue Burden (Rule 45(d))

Courts must quash or modify subpoenas that:

- Require appearance beyond geographic limits
- Require disclosure of privileged information
- Subject witnesses to undue burden or expense
- Require disclosure of trade secrets without protection

Document Production Procedures (Rule 45(e))

Document subpoenas must:

- Specify documents with reasonable particularity

- Allow reasonable time for production
- Designate reasonable times and places for inspection
- Provide for copying and return of original documents

Contempt Authority (Rule 45(g))

Failure to comply with subpoenas may result in:

- Contempt of court citations
- Monetary sanctions and attorney fee awards
- Other enforcement mechanisms available to courts

Practical Applications

1. Third-Party Discovery: Rule 45 enables discovery from non-party witnesses who possess relevant documents or information.
2. Expert Witness Compulsion: Adverse party experts may be subpoenaed for trial testimony when deposition testimony is insufficient.
3. Business Records: Non-party businesses can be compelled to produce relevant records through document subpoenas.

Strategic Considerations

1. Early Planning: Subpoena practice requires advance planning to meet service deadlines and coordinate witness schedules.

2. Burden Analysis: Subpoena requests must be proportional to case needs and witness capabilities to avoid protective motions.
3. Privilege Protection: Subpoenas must respect attorney-client privilege and other protected relationships.

Common Examination Issues

1. Geographic Limits: Students must calculate whether witnesses can be compelled to attend trial or depositions under Rule 45(c).
2. Burden Protection: Analyzing when subpoenas create undue burden requiring court intervention under Rule 45(d).
3. Service Requirements: Understanding personal service and witness fee obligations for effective subpoena practice.

RULE 46. OBJECTING TO A RULING OR ORDER

"A formal exception to a ruling or order is unnecessary. When the ruling or order is requested or made, a party need only state the grounds for taking exception to preserve a claim of error for appeal."

Core Requirements

Rule 46 simplifies error preservation by eliminating formal exception requirements while maintaining the necessity of stating objection grounds.

Error Preservation

1. Objection Timing: Parties must object when rulings are made or requested to preserve appellate issues.
2. Ground Specification: Objections must state specific grounds to inform courts of legal theories and preserve appellate arguments.
3. No Formal Language: Rule 46 eliminates the need for traditional "exception" language while maintaining substance requirements.

Waiver Prevention

1. Contemporaneous Objection: Failure to object timely waives most appellate arguments about trial court rulings.
2. Specificity Requirement: General objections may fail to preserve specific appellate arguments about legal errors.

Practical Applications

1. Trial Advocacy: Effective trial lawyers must object promptly to preserve clients' appellate rights while maintaining courtroom professionalism.
2. Evidentiary Rulings: Evidence objections require specific grounds (hearsay, relevance, privilege) to preserve appellate review.
3. Jury Instruction Challenges: Instruction objections must identify specific legal errors to support post-trial motions and appeals.

Strategic Considerations

1. Jury Impact: Frequent objections may harm jury perception, requiring strategic balance between error preservation and advocacy effectiveness.
2. Settlement Leverage: Preserved appellate issues can provide post-trial settlement leverage even after adverse verdicts.

RULE 47. SELECTING JURORS

"(a) Examining Jurors. The court may permit the parties or their attorneys to examine prospective jurors or may itself conduct the examination. In either event, the court may ask any questions it considers proper..."

Core Requirements

Rule 47 grants courts discretion over jury selection procedures while ensuring fair and impartial jury composition.

Examination Authority (Rule 47(a))

1. Court Discretion: Courts may conduct voir dire examination themselves or permit attorney questioning.
2. Question Control: Courts retain authority to determine appropriate questioning scope and methods.
3. Supplemental Questions: Courts may ask additional questions beyond party requests to ensure fair jury selection.

Challenge Types

1. Challenges for Cause: Unlimited challenges when prospective jurors demonstrate bias, relationship to parties, or other disqualifications.
2. Peremptory Challenges: Limited number of challenges without stated cause, typically three per side in civil cases.
3. Constitutional Limits: Peremptory challenges cannot be used to exclude jurors based on race, gender, or other protected characteristics.

Practical Applications

1. Bias Detection: Effective voir dire reveals potential juror biases that could affect fair trial rights.
2. Case Preparation: Jury selection provides insight into community attitudes and case presentation strategies.
3. Challenge Strategy: Strategic use of limited peremptory challenges requires careful evaluation of juror attitudes and case fit.

Strategic Considerations

1. Questioning Strategy: Effective voir dire balances information gathering with juror education about case themes.
2. Challenge Decisions: Peremptory challenge strategy requires prioritizing the most problematic jurors for exclusion.

Common Examination Issues

1. Challenge Standards: Students must distinguish between for-cause and peremptory challenges and their respective limitations.
2. Constitutional Violations: Understanding Batson challenges and other constitutional limits on jury selection practices.

RULE 48. NUMBER OF JURORS; VERDICT; POLLING

"(a) Number of Jurors. A jury must begin with at least 6 and no more than 12 members, and each juror must participate in the verdict unless excused under Rule 47(c)."

Core Requirements

Rule 48 establishes jury size and verdict requirements, providing flexibility while maintaining constitutional jury trial protections.

Jury Size (Rule 48(a))

1. Size Range: Federal civil juries must have at least 6 and no more than 12 members.
2. Participation Requirement: All sworn jurors must participate in verdict unless properly excused.
3. Court Discretion: Courts choose specific jury size within the permitted range based on case complexity and local practice.

Unanimous Verdict (Rule 48(b))

1. Unanimity Requirement: Civil jury verdicts must be unanimous unless parties stipulate otherwise.
2. Stipulated Majority: Parties may agree to accept majority verdicts with court approval.

Jury Polling (Rule 48(c))

1. Polling Rights: Any party may request jury polling after verdict announcement.
2. Individual Confirmation: Polling requires each juror to confirm their individual agreement with the verdict.
3. Dissent Consequences: If polling reveals disagreement, courts must send juries back for further deliberation or declare mistrial.

Practical Applications

1. Case Management: Jury size selection affects trial logistics, deliberation dynamics, and verdict predictability.
2. Verdict Security: Jury polling ensures verdict accuracy and prevents coercion or mistake in jury rooms.
3. Settlement Impact: Unanimity requirements may encourage settlement by increasing verdict uncertainty.

Strategic Considerations

1. Size Preferences: Larger juries may provide more diverse perspectives while smaller juries deliberate more efficiently.
2. Polling Strategy: Strategic polling decisions depend on verdict satisfaction and likelihood of jury dissent.

Common Examination Issues

1. Size Requirements: Understanding minimum and maximum jury size requirements and their constitutional basis.
2. Unanimity Analysis: Distinguishing civil jury unanimity requirements from criminal jury rules in various jurisdictions.

RULE 49. SPECIAL VERDICT; GENERAL VERDICT AND QUESTIONS

"(a) Special Verdict. The court may require a jury to return only a special verdict in the form of a written finding on each issue of fact. The court may do so by: (1) submitting written questions susceptible of a categorical or other brief answer..."

Core Requirements

Rule 49 provides alternatives to general verdicts through special verdicts and general verdicts with interrogatories, promoting accuracy and appellate review.

Special Verdicts (Rule 49(a))

1. Definition: Special verdicts require juries to make specific factual findings without rendering ultimate legal conclusions.

2. Question Format: Courts submit written questions requiring categorical answers about disputed factual issues.
3. Legal Application: Courts apply law to jury factual findings to determine judgment.

Advantages:

- Clearer appellate review of factual determinations
- Reduced inconsistent verdict risk
- Better understanding of jury reasoning
- Enhanced trial court control over legal conclusions

General Verdict with Interrogatories (Rule 49(b))

1. Combined Format: Juries render general verdicts accompanied by specific factual findings through interrogatories.
2. Consistency Review: Courts must examine verdict and interrogatory consistency before entering judgment.
3. Inconsistency Resolution: When verdicts and answers conflict, courts may enter judgment based on answers, order new trial, or return juries for further deliberation.

Practical Applications

1. Complex Cases: Special verdicts help juries navigate complicated factual issues with multiple legal theories.
2. Contributory Negligence: Personal injury cases often use special verdicts to separate liability, causation, and damage determinations.

3. Contract Disputes: Business cases may require specific findings about contract formation, performance, and breach elements.

Strategic Considerations

1. Jury Control: Special verdicts provide greater judicial control but may confuse juries with complex legal distinctions.
2. Appeal Planning: Special verdict findings create clearer appellate records for challenging legal applications to facts.
3. Settlement Timing: Special verdict procedures may delay resolution but provide more precise damage calculations.

Common Examination Issues

1. Inconsistency Analysis: Students must identify conflicts between general verdicts and interrogatory answers under Rule 49(b).
2. Question Drafting: Understanding how to formulate appropriate special verdict questions that avoid legal conclusions while eliciting necessary factual findings.

RULE 50. JUDGMENT AS A MATTER OF LAW IN A JURY TRIAL; RELATED MOTION FOR A NEW TRIAL; CONDITIONAL RULING

"(a) Judgment as a Matter of Law. (1) In General. If a party has been fully heard on an issue during a jury trial and the court finds that a reasonable jury would not have a legally sufficient evidentiary basis to find for the party on that issue, the court must grant a motion for judgment as a matter of law against that party on that issue."

Core Requirements

Rule 50 provides mechanisms for judicial intervention when evidence is legally insufficient to support jury verdicts, balancing jury trial rights with legal sufficiency standards.

Pre-Verdict Motion (Rule 50(a))

1. Timing: Motions may be made after opposing parties have been fully heard on relevant issues.
2. Standard: Courts must find that reasonable juries would lack legally sufficient evidentiary basis for party findings.
3. Preservation: Pre-verdict motions preserve post-verdict motion rights under Rule 50(b).

Legal Sufficiency Test:

- View evidence in light most favorable to non-moving party

- Draw all reasonable inferences for non-moving party
- Consider only evidence supporting non-moving party's position
- Apply reasonable jury standard, not court's view of evidence weight

Post-Verdict Motion (Rule 50(b))

1. Timing Requirement: Motions must be filed within 28 days after judgment entry.
2. Prior Motion Prerequisite: Post-verdict motions require prior Rule 50(a) motions on the same issues.
3. New Trial Alternative: Rule 50(b) motions may include alternative new trial requests under Rule 59.

Conditional Rulings (Rule 50(c))

When courts conditionally grant or deny post-verdict motions, they may:

- Grant judgment as a matter of law while conditionally ruling on new trial motions
- Deny judgment as a matter of law while conditionally granting new trial if appellate court reverses
- Provide alternative rulings for different appeal outcomes

Standards for Granting

1. Directed Verdict Standard: Evidence must be so one-sided that reasonable people could not disagree about outcome.
2. Credibility Issues: Courts cannot weigh witness credibility or resolve conflicting evidence.
3. Inference Limitations: All reasonable inferences must favor the non-moving party.

Practical Applications

1. Product Liability: Insufficient causation evidence may support judgment as a matter of law against plaintiff claims.
2. Contract Cases: Clear contract language may require judgment as a matter of law on interpretation issues.
3. Employment Discrimination: Lack of evidence supporting discrimination claims may justify employer judgment motions.

Strategic Considerations

1. Motion Timing: Strategic Rule 50(a) motion timing balances preservation needs with jury impact concerns.
2. Appellate Strategy: Conditional rulings provide appellate alternatives and may encourage favorable settlements.

3. Evidence Development: Anticipating Rule 50 challenges requires thorough evidence development during discovery and trial.

Common Examination Issues

1. Legal Sufficiency Analysis: Students must apply the reasonable jury standard while viewing evidence favorably to non-moving parties.
2. Timing Requirements: Understanding pre-verdict motion requirements for preserving post-verdict motion rights.
3. Conditional Ruling Effects: Analyzing how conditional rulings interact with appellate outcomes and final judgment options.

RULE 51. INSTRUCTIONS TO THE JURY; OBJECTIONS; PRESERVING A CLAIM OF ERROR

"(a) Requests. (1) Before or at the Close of the Evidence. At the close of the evidence or at any earlier reasonable time that the court orders, a party may file and furnish to every other party written requests for the jury instructions it wants the court to give."

Core Requirements

Rule 51 governs jury instruction procedures, including request requirements, objection standards, and error preservation mechanisms.

Instruction Requests (Rule 51(a))

1. Timing: Parties must submit written instruction requests before evidence closes or at court-ordered earlier times.
2. Content Requirements: Requests must be written and furnished to all parties.
3. Court Discretion: Courts may accept late requests for good cause but are not required to consider untimely submissions.

Court Obligations (Rule 51(b))

1. Instruction Conference: Courts must inform parties of proposed instructions and give parties opportunity to object before final argument.
2. Objection Opportunity: Parties must have reasonable opportunity to object to proposed instructions and request modifications.
3. Record Creation: Courts must create adequate records of instruction disputes for appellate review.

Objection Requirements (Rule 51(c))

Timing Options: Parties may object to instructions:

- Before instructions are given to jury
- After instructions are given but before jury deliberation begins

Specificity: Objections must state specific grounds and proposed alternatives to preserve error for appeal.

Error Preservation (Rule 51(d))

1. Requested Instructions: Parties who properly request instructions and object to refusals preserve error for appeal.
2. Unrequested Instructions: Parties may preserve error about unrequested instructions by timely objection after instructions are given.
3. Plain Error: Courts may recognize plain error in jury instructions even without proper objection.

Practical Applications

1. Legal Theory Protection: Proper instruction requests ensure juries receive accurate legal standards for case evaluation.
2. Verdict Direction: Strategic instruction requests can influence jury understanding of legal requirements and evidence evaluation.

3. Appeal Preservation: Careful instruction practice preserves post-trial motion and appellate rights.

Strategic Considerations

1. Instruction Strategy: Effective instruction requests require balancing comprehensive legal coverage with jury comprehension.
2. Objection Timing: Strategic objection timing considers jury impact and preservation requirements.
3. Settlement Leverage: Instruction disputes may provide post-trial settlement leverage through preserved appellate issues.

Common Examination Issues

1. Error Preservation: Students must understand different preservation requirements for requested versus unrequested instruction errors.
2. Objection Standards: Analyzing adequacy of instruction objections for appellate preservation purposes.
3. Plain Error Analysis: Understanding when appellate courts may address instruction errors despite inadequate preservation.

RULE 52. FINDINGS AND CONCLUSIONS BY THE COURT; JUDGMENT ON PARTIAL FINDINGS

"(a) In General. In an action tried on the facts without a jury or with an advisory jury, the court must find the facts specially and state its conclusions of law separately..."

Core Requirements

Rule 52 mandates specific factual findings and legal conclusions in bench trials, facilitating appellate review and ensuring thorough judicial analysis.

Findings Requirement (Rule 52(a))

1. Bench Trials: Courts must make specific factual findings and separate legal conclusions in non-jury trials.
2. Advisory Jury Cases: When advisory juries are used, courts still must make independent findings and conclusions.
3. Sufficiency Standard: Findings must be sufficient to enable appellate courts to understand factual and legal bases for judgments.

Content Requirements

1. Factual Findings: Specific findings about disputed material facts based on evidence presented at trial.
2. Legal Conclusions: Separate statements of legal principles applied to factual findings.

3. Credibility Determinations: Courts should explain credibility assessments when witness testimony conflicts.
4. Evidentiary Analysis: Findings should demonstrate consideration of all relevant evidence and explain weight given to different sources.

Timing and Amendment (Rule 52(b))

1. Initial Findings: Courts may state findings and conclusions orally after trial or in written post-trial orders.
2. Amendment Authority: Courts may amend findings and conclusions to correct clear error or address omitted issues.
3. Timing Limits: Amendments must be made promptly, typically within the time for post-trial motions.

Appellate Review Standards

1. Factual Findings: Clear error standard applies to factual determinations, giving substantial deference to trial courts.
2. Legal Conclusions: De novo review applies to pure legal conclusions and mixed questions of law and fact.
3. Credibility Findings: Great deference given to trial court credibility determinations based on demeanor observation.

Judgment on Partial Findings (Rule 52(c))

1. Early Resolution: In bench trials, parties may move for judgment on partial findings after opposing parties have presented evidence on specific issues.
2. Standards: Same legal sufficiency standards as Rule 50 motions in jury trials.
3. Efficiency Benefits: Allows resolution of clear cases without completing lengthy bench trials.

Practical Applications

1. Complex Commercial Cases: Detailed findings help appellate courts review intricate business disputes and regulatory compliance issues.
2. Family Law Matters: Custody and support determinations require specific findings about children's best interests and financial circumstances.
3. Patent Litigation: Technical patent cases benefit from detailed findings about claim construction and infringement analysis.

Strategic Considerations

1. Finding Requests: Parties may request specific findings on particular issues to ensure adequate appellate record development.
2. Evidence Presentation: Bench trial advocacy must focus on creating clear record for factual findings rather than jury persuasion.

3. Appeal Planning: Detailed findings help identify viable appellate issues while comprehensive coverage may limit appeal grounds.

Common Examination Issues

1. Clear Error Standard: Students must understand the deferential appellate review standard for factual findings in bench trials.
2. Finding Adequacy: Analyzing whether trial court findings are sufficiently specific for meaningful appellate review.
3. Legal vs. Factual Determinations: Distinguishing between factual findings receiving deference and legal conclusions reviewed de novo.

RULE 53. MASTERS

"(a) Appointment. (1) Scope. Unless a statute provides otherwise, a court may appoint a master only to: (A) perform duties consented to by the parties; (B) hold trial proceedings and make or recommend findings of fact on issues to be decided without a jury if appointment is warranted by: (i) some exceptional condition..."

Core Requirements

Rule 53 provides authority for appointing special masters to assist with complex litigation, subject to strict limitations and procedural safeguards.

Appointment Standards (Rule 53(a))

Limited Authority: Masters may be appointed only for:

- Duties consented to by parties
- Exceptional circumstances requiring special expertise
- Complex accounting or technical issues
- Pre-trial and post-trial matters where master assistance benefits case management

Exceptional Condition Requirement: Non-consensual appointments require showing that appointment is warranted by exceptional circumstances making master reference appropriate.

Master Categories

1. Special Masters: Handle specific discrete tasks like discovery disputes or technical issue resolution.
2. Trial Masters: Conduct trial proceedings in exceptional circumstances, typically with party consent.
3. Accounting Masters: Address complex financial calculations and audit issues in business litigation.

Appointment Process (Rule 53(b))

1. Court Order Required: Master appointments require specific court orders defining scope, powers, and compensation.
2. Qualifications: Masters must possess appropriate expertise for assigned tasks and be free from disqualifying conflicts.
3. Compensation Terms: Appointment orders must address master compensation and cost allocation among parties.

Master Powers and Duties (Rule 53(c))

1. Authority Scope: Masters possess only powers specifically granted in appointment orders.
2. Procedural Authority: Masters may regulate proceedings, take evidence, and make procedural rulings within their mandate.
3. Report Requirements: Masters must prepare detailed reports with findings and recommendations for court consideration.

Review of Master Decisions (Rule 53(f))

1. Factual Findings: Master factual findings in non-jury matters are reviewed for clear error unless parties stipulate otherwise.
2. Legal Conclusions: Courts review master legal conclusions de novo.

3. Procedural Rulings: Master procedural decisions receive abuse of discretion review.

Objections and Review (Rule 53(g))

1. Objection Requirements: Parties must timely object to master reports to preserve review rights.
2. Hearing Rights: Courts must provide reasonable opportunity to be heard on master report objections.
3. Adoption Standards: Courts may adopt, modify, or reject master reports based on objection analysis and independent review.

Practical Applications

1. Discovery Disputes: Masters help resolve complex electronic discovery disputes and privilege issues in large cases.
2. Accounting Issues: Business valuation and damages calculation cases benefit from master expertise in financial analysis.
3. Technical Matters: Patent, construction, and environmental cases may require masters with specialized technical knowledge.
4. Case Management: Complex multi-party litigation may benefit from master assistance with scheduling and coordination.

Strategic Considerations

1. Cost-Benefit Analysis: Master appointments involve significant costs that must be justified by case complexity and efficiency benefits.
2. Expert Selection: Master selection requires careful evaluation of expertise, neutrality, and case-specific qualifications.
3. Appeal Strategy: Master findings create different appellate standards depending on whether issues are factual or legal.

Common Examination Issues

1. Appointment Standards: Students must understand when exceptional circumstances justify non-consensual master appointments.
2. Review Standards: Analyzing different appellate review standards for master factual findings versus legal conclusions.
3. Procedural Requirements: Understanding objection and review procedures for master reports and recommendations.

TRIAL PRACTICE INTEGRATION

Pre-Trial Preparation

Effective trial practice requires comprehensive preparation integrating multiple rule requirements:

- Witness preparation coordinated with subpoena and scheduling requirements
- Exhibit preparation following authentication and foundation rules
- Jury instruction development beginning early in case development
- Settlement negotiations informed by trial readiness and evidence strength

Evidence Presentation Strategy

Trial advocacy must account for rule-based procedural requirements:

- Witness examination techniques adapted to live testimony preferences under Rule 43
- Document authentication procedures following Rules 44 and 45
- Expert witness presentation coordinated with disclosure requirements
- Objection practices balancing error preservation with jury relations

Case Management Coordination

Trial rules interact significantly with case management requirements:

- Discovery completion deadlines affect trial preparation timing

- Motion practice resolution influences trial strategy development
- Settlement conference scheduling coordinates with trial calendar management
- Appeal planning begins during trial through proper objection and error preservation

Technology Integration in Modern Trials

Contemporary trial practice increasingly incorporates technology within traditional rule frameworks:

- Video deposition presentation equipment and procedures
- Electronic exhibit management systems for document-intensive cases
- Real-time court reporting and transcript access for complex proceedings
- Remote witness testimony technology for international or unavailable witnesses

Post-Trial Considerations

Trial rules establish foundations for post-trial proceedings:

- Rule 50 and 59 motion practice requires proper pre-trial preservation
- Appeal planning depends on adequate error preservation during trial

- Settlement negotiations may continue after verdict based on post-trial motion prospects
- Enforcement planning begins with judgment entry and appellate deadline calculations

The trial rules create a comprehensive framework balancing constitutional jury trial rights with judicial efficiency and case management needs. Understanding these rules enables effective advocacy while preserving client rights and appeal options. Modern trial practice requires integrating traditional advocacy skills with technological capabilities and sophisticated understanding of procedural requirements that can determine case outcomes independent of substantive merits.

TITLE VII - JUDGMENT

Title VII represents the culmination of federal civil litigation, governing how courts enter, modify, and provide relief from judgments. These ten rules (Rules 54-63) address everything from calculating costs and default judgments to summary judgment practice and post-trial relief. Understanding Title VII is essential for effective litigation practice, as these rules determine when cases truly end and what remedies parties may obtain. The rules balance finality principles with fairness concerns, providing mechanisms for correcting errors while maintaining judicial efficiency and party expectations.

RULE 54. JUDGMENT; COSTS

Rule 54 defines "judgment" and establishes the framework for awarding costs to prevailing parties, while addressing timing issues for multiple claims and parties.

Judgment Definition (Rule 54(a))

Rule 54(a) provides a broad definition that includes any final decision disposing of all claims against all parties. This includes:

- Final judgments after trial on the merits
- Summary judgments disposing of entire cases

- Dismissals with prejudice that resolve all claims
- Default judgments against all defendants

The rule clarifies that "judgment" encompasses decrees and any order from which an appeal lies, ensuring comprehensive coverage of final dispositive rulings.

Costs Award (Rule 54(d))

Rule 54(d) establishes the presumption that prevailing parties recover costs from losing parties:

1. Default Rule: Unless statute, rule, or court order provides otherwise, costs other than attorney fees shall be allowed to the prevailing party.
2. Taxation Process: The clerk taxes costs on 14 days' notice, subject to court review on motion served within seven days.
3. Attorney Fees Exception: Attorney fees are not included in "costs" unless specifically authorized by statute, rule, or agreement.

Costs Categories

Recoverable costs typically include:

- Filing fees and court reporter fees
- Process service costs
- Witness fees and travel expenses
- Copying costs for exhibits and depositions
- Translation costs for foreign language documents

Non-recoverable items generally include:

- Attorney fees (unless statutorily authorized)
- Investigative expenses
- Internal copying and administrative costs
- Travel and lodging for attorneys
- Expert witness fees beyond statutory limits

Multiple Claims and Parties (Rule 54(b))

Rule 54(b) addresses timing for appeals when cases involve multiple claims or parties:

Final Judgment Requirement: Ordinarily, only final judgments disposing of all claims against all parties are appealable.

Partial Final Judgment: Courts may direct entry of final judgment on fewer than all claims only when:

- No just reason exists for delay
- Court makes express determination that immediate appeal is appropriate
- Court expressly directs entry of judgment under Rule 54(b)

Strategic Importance: Rule 54(b) certification allows immediate appeal of resolved claims while related litigation continues, preventing unnecessary delay in obtaining appellate review.

Practical Applications

Cost Recovery Strategy

Effective cost management requires:

- Maintaining detailed records of all taxable expenses
- Distinguishing between recoverable costs and non-recoverable attorney work product
- Understanding local court practices for cost taxation
- Timely filing cost bills within applicable deadlines

Rule 54(b) Considerations

Courts analyze several factors when considering Rule 54(b) certification:

- Relationship between resolved and pending claims
- Possibility that trial court findings may be altered by further proceedings
- Risk of duplicative appeals if certification is denied
- Hardship to parties from delayed appeal

Appeals Strategy

Rule 54(b) certification can be crucial for:

- Cases where early liability determinations affect settlement negotiations
- Situations where immediate appellate review could dispose of entire litigation

- Complex multi-party litigation where piecemeal resolution serves efficiency

Strategic Considerations

Cost-Benefit Analysis

Parties must weigh cost recovery potential against:

- Relationship preservation with opposing parties
- Administrative burden of cost documentation
- Risk of reciprocal cost liability if positions are reversed on appeal
- Settlement negotiation implications

Settlement Impact

Cost liability often influences settlement discussions, particularly when:

- Potential cost awards approach or exceed underlying damages
- Multiple parties create complex cost allocation issues
- Statutory attorney fee provisions create additional exposure

Common Pitfalls

Incomplete Cost Documentation

Failure to maintain contemporaneous records of taxable costs creates recovery difficulties. Best practices include:

- Segregating taxable costs from general litigation expenses
- Obtaining detailed invoices from service providers
- Creating audit trails for expense categorization
- Understanding local court limitations and requirements

Rule 54(b) Misapplication

Courts strictly construe Rule 54(b) requirements. Common errors include:

- Seeking certification for interlocutory rulings rather than final judgments on specific claims
- Failing to demonstrate absence of just reason for delay
- Inadequate briefing on relationship between certified and remaining claims

RULE 55. DEFAULT; DEFAULT JUDGMENT

Rule 55 establishes the process for obtaining default judgments when defendants fail to appear or respond to complaints within required time limits.

Core Requirements

Entry of Default (Rule 55(a))

When a party against whom judgment is sought has failed to plead or otherwise defend, the clerk must enter default upon affidavit showing the failure.

a) Automatic Process: Clerk's entry of default is largely ministerial when proper documentation is provided.
b) Time Requirements: Default typically follows expiration of Rule 12 response periods without defendant action.
c) Notice Issues: Plaintiff must establish that defendant received adequate notice of the proceedings.

Default Judgment Process (Rule 55(b))

Rule 55(b) provides two pathways for obtaining default judgment:

Clerk's Default Judgment (Rule 55(b)(1))

The clerk may enter judgment for a sum certain or amount that can be calculated with mathematical certainty when:

- Defendant is not an infant or incompetent person
- Defendant has not appeared in the action
- Default has been entered
- Affidavit establishes amount owed with specificity

Court's Default Judgment (Rule 55(b)(2))

In all other cases, the court must enter default judgment. This includes:

- Claims for unliquidated damages
- Cases involving incompetent persons or minors
- Situations where defendants have appeared but failed to respond
- Complex damages requiring court determination

Notice and Hearing Requirements

Notice to Appearing Defendants

If defendant has appeared personally or through counsel, at least 7 days' written notice of default judgment application is required.

Hearing Requirements

Courts may conduct hearings to:

- Establish damages when amount is unclear
- Ensure jurisdiction and proper service
- Consider defendant's interests when default results from excusable neglect
- Determine appropriate relief when multiple remedies are requested

Damages in Default Cases

Liquidated Damages

For claims seeking specific monetary amounts (contract breaches, promissory notes), clerks may enter judgment for the precise sum demanded plus costs and interest.

Unliquidated Damages

For tort claims, unliquidated contract damages, or equitable relief, courts must determine appropriate awards through:

- Document review and affidavit evidence
- Limited hearings with witness testimony

- Damage calculation based on pleading limitations
- Consideration of plaintiff's mitigation efforts

Pleading Limitations

Default judgments cannot exceed relief demanded in pleadings except for costs, interest, and attorney fees where authorized by statute or contract.

Setting Aside Default (Rule 55(c))

Standards for Relief

Courts may set aside defaults for good cause shown, considering:

- Whether default resulted from excusable neglect
- Promptness of motion to set aside
- Merit of defendant's proposed defense
- Prejudice to plaintiff from delay

Timing Considerations

While no specific deadline exists, defendants must act promptly after discovering default. Extended delay without justification reduces likelihood of relief.

Default Judgment Relief

Setting aside default judgments requires meeting Rule 60(b) standards, which are more stringent than Rule 55(c) requirements for setting aside mere entries of default.

Strategic Applications

Plaintiff Strategy

Effective default practice includes:

- Ensuring proper service documentation
- Maintaining detailed damage calculations
- Preparing for potential set-aside motions
- Understanding collection enforcement options

Defense Considerations

When facing default:

- Acting immediately upon notice discovery
- Developing compelling excusable neglect arguments
- Demonstrating meritorious defenses
- Showing minimal prejudice to opponents

Common Examination Issues

1. Service Requirements: Students must understand that default judgments require valid service of process. Insufficient service notice voids resulting judgments.
2. Damages Limitations: Exam questions often test understanding that default judgments cannot exceed pleading demands, requiring careful complaint drafting.
3. Set-Aside Standards: Distinguishing between standards for setting aside defaults versus default judgments frequently appears on examinations.

RULE 56. SUMMARY JUDGMENT

Rule 56 provides the mechanism for resolving cases without trial when no genuine dispute of material fact exists and the moving party is entitled to judgment as a matter of law.

Core Requirements

Standard for Summary Judgment (Rule 56(a))

Courts shall grant summary judgment if the movant shows that there is no genuine dispute as to any material fact and the movant is entitled to judgment as a matter of law.

a) Material Fact: Facts that could affect the outcome under applicable substantive law.
b) Genuine Dispute: Disputes where reasonable juries could reach different conclusions based on available evidence.
c) Legal Entitlement: Even undisputed facts must legally support the requested judgment

Timing Requirements (Rule 56(b))

Unless court orders otherwise or local rules provide different timing:

- Any party may move for summary judgment at any time until 30 days after close of all discovery
- Courts may set different deadlines through case management orders
- Courts may grant summary judgment sua sponte after notice and reasonable opportunity to respond

Supporting Materials (Rule 56(c))

Proper Support

Parties must support assertions by citing to:

- Depositions, documents, electronically stored information, affidavits, declarations, stipulations, admissions, interrogatory answers, or other materials in the record
- Materials must be authenticated and admissible in form

Opposition Requirements

Non-movants must go beyond pleadings and provide:

- Specific facts showing genuine dispute for trial
- Evidence that would be admissible at trial
- More than "mere allegations or denials" of moving party's assertions

Affidavit Standards (Rule 56(c)(4))

Supporting affidavits must:

- Be made on personal knowledge
- Set out facts that would be admissible in evidence
- Show that declarant is competent to testify about stated matters

Procedural Framework

Burden Structure

a) Initial Burden: Moving party must show absence of genuine factual disputes
b) Response Burden: Non-moving party must demonstrate specific factual disputes
c) Legal Standards: Courts view evidence in light most favorable to non-moving party

Partial Summary Judgment (Rule 56(g))

When full summary judgment is inappropriate, courts may:

- Grant partial summary judgment on specific issues
- Establish facts not genuinely in dispute
- Limit trial scope to remaining disputed issues
- Issue orders specifying established facts

Strategic Applications

Timing Considerations

Effective summary judgment practice requires:

- Completing sufficient discovery to support motion
- Understanding opponent's likely evidence sources
- Coordinating motion timing with case management deadlines
- Considering settlement leverage from strong motions

Motion Crafting

Successful motions typically:

- Focus on single, dispositive legal theory
- Organize facts clearly with record citations
- Anticipate and address opponent's strongest arguments
- Provide clear legal analysis applying undisputed facts

Opposition Strategy

Effective opposition includes:

- Identifying all factual disputes with specific record citations
- Demonstrating that disputed facts are material to legal claims
- Showing that reasonable juries could find in non-movant's favor
- Requesting additional discovery time when appropriate

Substantive Law Integration

Different Claim Types

Summary judgment analysis varies by claim type:

a) Contract Claims: Focus on contract terms, performance, and breach
b) Tort Claims: Analyze duty, breach, causation, and damages elements
c) Constitutional Claims: Consider qualified immunity and constitutional standards

d) Employment Claims: Address discrimination, retaliation, and procedural compliance

Burden of Proof Considerations

Courts consider ultimate trial burdens when evaluating summary judgment:

- Parties with trial burdens face higher summary judgment hurdles
- Defendants may obtain summary judgment by showing plaintiff cannot prove essential elements
- Affirmative defenses require defendants to establish undisputed factual foundations

Common Pitfalls

Discovery Insufficiency

Premature summary judgment motions often fail when:

- Key witness depositions remain incomplete
- Document production is ongoing
- Expert discovery has not concluded
- Opponent's evidence sources are not fully explored

Legal Standard Misapplication

Common errors include:

- Weighing evidence rather than determining dispute existence
- Resolving credibility issues inappropriate for summary judgment

- Applying incorrect legal standards to undisputed facts
- Failing to view evidence favorably to non-movants

Practical Impact

Case Management Benefits

Summary judgment practice provides:

- Early resolution of meritless claims
- Cost savings through avoided trial preparation
- Judicial efficiency in managing docket
- Settlement leverage from motion outcomes

Strategic Settlement Tool

Strong summary judgment motions often prompt:

- Renewed settlement discussions
- Realistic case valuation by opponents
- Resolution timing pressure
- Cost-benefit recalculation by parties

RULE 57. DECLARATORY JUDGMENT

Rule 57 provides the procedural framework for declaratory judgment actions, allowing courts to declare parties' rights and legal relations without ordering specific performance.

Core Requirements

Scope and Purpose

Declaratory judgments determine legal rights and relations without requiring further relief. They are particularly valuable for:

- Resolving uncertainty about legal obligations
- Preventing larger disputes through early clarification
- Insurance coverage disputes
- Contract interpretation questions
- Constitutional challenges to statutes or regulations

Integration with Other Remedies

Rule 57 permits declaratory relief as the sole remedy or in combination with coercive relief. Courts may:

- Grant only declaratory judgment when appropriate
- Combine declarations with injunctive relief
- Order further proceedings after declaratory determinations
- Provide declaratory relief as predicate for damages awards

Statutory Foundation

Rule 57 implements the Federal Declaratory Judgment Act (28 U.S.C. §§ 2201-2202), which grants district courts discretion to declare rights in "cases of actual controversy."

1. Actual Controversy Requirement: Courts require genuine disputes about legal rights, not hypothetical questions or advisory opinions.
2. Jurisdictional Independence: Declaratory judgment actions must independently satisfy federal jurisdictional requirements; the remedy itself does not create federal question jurisdiction.

Practical Applications

Insurance Coverage

Declaratory judgments commonly resolve:

- Duty to defend questions in liability policies
- Coverage scope under property insurance
- Exclusion applicability disputes
- Multiple insurer obligations in complex claims

Contract Disputes

Parties frequently seek declarations regarding:

- Contract interpretation and meaning
- Performance obligations under agreements
- Breach consequences and remedies
- Modification and termination rights

Intellectual Property

Declaratory judgment actions address:

- Patent validity and infringement questions
- Trademark rights and priority

- Copyright ownership and licensing scope
- Trade secret protection boundaries

Strategic Considerations

Timing Advantages

- Declaratory judgment actions often provide:
- Early resolution before damages accumulate
- Forum selection opportunities for plaintiffs
- Cost-effective dispute resolution
- Settlement leverage through legal clarification

Discretionary Denial

- Courts may decline declaratory relief when:
- Coercive action is pending in another forum
- State court proceedings address identical issues
- Administrative processes should be exhausted first
- Declaration would not resolve practical controversies

Common Pitfalls

Abstention Doctrines

Federal courts may abstain from declaratory judgment actions involving:

- Ongoing state court proceedings
- State law questions of uncertain meaning
- Administrative enforcement actions
- Local government regulation challenges

Practical Resolution

Courts sometimes deny declaratory relief when:

- Parties' conduct has resolved underlying disputes
- Changed circumstances eliminate controversy
- Declaration would not guide future behavior
- Coercive remedies are more appropriate

RULE 58. ENTERING JUDGMENT

Rule 58 establishes requirements for entering judgments and determines when judgments become effective for appeal and enforcement purposes.

Core Requirements

Separate Document Rule (Rule 58(a))

Every judgment must be set out in a separate document, distinct from any opinion, order, or other court writing.

a) Clarity Requirement: Judgments must be self-contained and clearly state the relief granted.
b) Finality Purpose: Separate documents provide clear notice of case resolution and appeal timing.
c) Integration with Rule 79: Clerk must enter judgments in civil docket per Rule 79 requirements.

Entry Timing (Rule 58(b))

Judgment entry occurs when:

- Judgment is set out in separate document and entered in civil docket, or
- 150 days have run from entry in civil docket of order disposing of all claims

Automatic Entry (Rule 58(c))

Clerk must prepare, sign, and enter judgment without court order when:

- Jury returns general verdict
- Court awards only costs or combination of costs, attorney fees, and interest
- Court denies all relief

Timing Implications

Appeal Deadlines

Rule 58 directly affects Federal Rule of Appellate Procedure timing:

- Appeal time runs from judgment entry, not from underlying court decisions
- Premature appeals are typically dismissed for lack of jurisdiction
- Post-judgment motions may extend or restart appeal timing

Enforcement Rights

Judgment entry triggers:

- Rule 69 execution rights

- Rule 62 stay considerations
- Rule 60 relief timing for certain grounds
- Interest accrual on monetary judgments

Strategic Applications

Monitoring Judgment Entry

Effective practice requires:

- Tracking judgment entry dates carefully
- Ensuring compliance with separate document requirements
- Understanding interaction with post-judgment motion timing
- Preparing for immediate enforcement or appeal deadlines

Drafting Considerations

Proper judgment drafting includes:

- Clear statement of relief granted to each party
- Specific monetary amounts and payment terms
- Injunctive relief language that is enforceable
- Cost and attorney fee determinations when appropriate

Common Issues

Separate Document Failures

Frequent problems include:

- Orders that dispose of cases without separate judgment documents
- Judgments incorporated into lengthy opinions
- Unclear relief statements that complicate enforcement
- Missing entries in civil dockets

Timing Confusion

Practitioners often struggle with:

- Distinguishing between order dates and judgment entry dates
- Understanding 150-day fallback provisions
- Coordinating post-judgment motions with appeal deadlines
- Managing enforcement timing with potential appeals

RULE 59. NEW TRIAL; ALTERING OR AMENDING A JUDGMENT

Rule 59 provides mechanisms for obtaining new trials and altering or amending judgments through post-trial motions that must be filed within strict time limits.

Core Requirements

New Trial Grounds (Rule 59(a))

Courts may grant new trials to any party for reasons including:

- Irregularities in proceedings or court orders that prevented fair trials

- Misconduct by prevailing parties, attorneys, or jury members
- Accident or surprise that ordinary prudence could not guard against
- Newly discovered evidence that could not have been discovered with due diligence before trial
- Excessive or inadequate damages appearing to have resulted from passion or prejudice
- Insufficiency of evidence to justify verdicts
- Errors in law during trial proceedings

Types of New Trials

Courts may grant:

- Complete new trials on all issues
- Partial new trials limited to specific issues
- New trials conditioned on damage remittitur or additur
- New trials limited to damages when liability is established

Altering or Amending Judgments (Rule 59(e))

Rule 59(e) motions may seek to:

- Correct clear errors of law or fact
- Address newly discovered evidence
- Respond to intervening changes in controlling law
- Prevent manifest injustice

Timing Requirements

Strict Deadlines (Rule 59(b) and (e))

- New trial motions must be filed no later than 28 days after judgment entry
- Motions to alter or amend must be filed no later than 28 days after judgment entry
- Courts cannot extend these deadlines under Rule 6(b)
- Premature motions are treated as filed on judgment entry date

Court Initiative (Rule 59(d))

Courts may order new trials on their own initiative within 28 days after judgment entry, but must give parties notice and opportunity to be heard.

Standards for Relief

New Trial Standards

Different standards apply based on trial type:

a) Jury Trials: Courts may not grant new trials unless verdict is against clear weight of evidence
b) Bench Trials: Courts have broader discretion to reconsider factual findings
c) Mixed Issues: Legal errors require new trials; factual errors depend on prejudicial impact

Rule 59(e) Standards

Courts typically grant Rule 59(e) motions only for:

- Clear errors of law or fact
- Newly discovered evidence meeting strict criteria
- Manifest injustice prevention
- Intervening controlling authority changes

High Bar: Rule 59(e) is not for relitigating issues or presenting previously available arguments.

Practical Applications

Strategic Timing

Rule 59 motions serve multiple purposes:

- Preserving appeal rights through objection preservation
- Seeking cost-effective relief compared to appeals
- Buying time for settlement negotiations
- Testing strength of opponents' cases

Evidence Considerations

New trial motions often focus on:

- Jury instruction errors that affected verdict
- Evidence rulings that improperly excluded or admitted material
- Conduct by attorneys or parties that prejudiced proceedings
- Newly discovered evidence that changes case outcomes

Integration with Appeals

Appellate Impact

Rule 59 motions affect appeals by:

- Extending time for filing appeals under FRAP 4
- Preserving issues for appellate review
- Potentially mooting appeals through favorable district court rulings
- Creating additional appellate issues if motions are denied

Strategic Considerations

Parties must balance:

- Likelihood of district court relief versus appellate success
- Cost and time considerations for extended litigation
- Settlement leverage from pending post-trial motions
- Risk of adverse appellate jurisdiction timing

Common Pitfalls

Timing Errors

Frequent mistakes include:

- Calculating deadlines from order dates rather than judgment entry
- Assuming courts can extend Rule 59 deadlines
- Filing premature motions before proper judgment entry

- Missing deadlines due to separate document rule confusion

Substantive Standards

Common errors involve:

- Using Rule 59(e) to relitigate previously decided issues
- Failing to meet high standards for newly discovered evidence
- Misunderstanding different standards for jury versus bench trials
- Inadequate preservation of trial objections

RULE 60. RELIEF FROM A JUDGMENT OR ORDER

Rule 60 provides mechanisms for obtaining relief from final judgments and orders, balancing finality principles with justice considerations through both time-limited and continuing grounds for relief.

Core Requirements

Two Categories of Relief

Rule 60 establishes distinct pathways for post-judgment relief with different timing and substantive requirements.

Rule 60(b)(1)-(3): Time-Limited Grounds

These grounds require motions within one year of judgment entry:

Rule 60(b)(1) - Mistake, Inadvertence, Surprise, Excusable Neglect

- Covers attorney errors, calendaring mistakes, and reasonable oversights
- Requires showing that mistake was excusable under circumstances
- Balances diligence expectations with fairness concerns

Rule 60(b)(2) - Newly Discovered Evidence

- Evidence must have existed at time of judgment
- Must show due diligence could not have discovered evidence earlier
- Evidence must be material and likely to change result
- Perjury and fraud claims often invoke this ground

Rule 60(b)(3) - Fraud, Misrepresentation, Misconduct

- Covers opponent fraud, perjury, or misconduct affecting judgment
- Requires clear and convincing evidence of misconduct
- Must show misconduct prevented fair adjudication
- Distinguished from mere false testimony or erroneous evidence

Rule 60(b)(4)-(6): Continuing Grounds

These grounds have no time limit but require "reasonable time" for filing:

Rule 60(b)(4) - Void Judgments

- Judgments void for lack of jurisdiction over subject matter or person
- Judgments exceeding court's power
- Due process violations in obtaining judgment
- Only ground that makes judgments absolutely void

Rule 60(b)(5) - Prospective Application Issues

- Changed circumstances making continued enforcement inequitable
- Supervening law changes affecting judgment validity
- Primary application to injunctive and continuing relief
- Forward-looking rather than backward-looking relief

Rule 60(b)(6) - Extraordinary Circumstances

- Catchall provision for unusual situations not covered by other grounds
- Requires truly exceptional circumstances justifying relief
- High burden requiring compelling equity considerations
- Cannot be used to circumvent other grounds' requirements

Timing Requirements

One-Year Deadline (Rule 60(c)(1))

Motions under Rule 60(b)(1), (2), and (3) must be made within one year of judgment entry. This deadline is jurisdictional and cannot be extended.

Reasonable Time Standard (Rule 60(c)(1))

Motions under Rule 60(b)(4), (5), and (6) must be made within reasonable time, considering:

- Length of delay after judgment
- Prejudice to opposing parties
- Reason for delay in seeking relief
- Changed circumstances since judgment

Standards for Relief

Diligence Requirements

All Rule 60(b) grounds require showing reasonable diligence in:

- Discovering grounds for relief
- Pursuing available remedies
- Filing motions promptly after discovery
- Meeting procedural requirements

Exceptional Circumstances Test

Courts apply strict scrutiny requiring:

- Compelling reasons justifying relief from final judgment
- Balance between finality principles and justice concerns
- Clear showing that alternative remedies are inadequate
- Demonstration that continued enforcement would be inequitable

Practical Applications

Fraud and Misconduct Cases

Rule 60(b)(3) commonly applies to:

- Opposing counsel's discovery violations
- Witness perjury affecting trial outcomes
- Document concealment or destruction
- Attorney conflicts of interest

Changed Circumstances

Rule 60(b)(5) addresses situations where:

- New law invalidates previous judgment basis
- Factual changes make continued enforcement inappropriate
- Constitutional decisions affect judgment validity
- Regulatory changes alter legal landscape

Extraordinary Circumstances

Rule 60(b)(6) covers unusual cases such as:

- Attorney abandonment of clients
- Serious due process violations
- Imprisonment preventing adequate representation
- Natural disasters affecting litigation

Strategic Considerations

Relationship to Appeals

Rule 60 motions interact complexly with appeals:

- Filing Rule 60 motion may waive appeal rights in some circumstances
- Motions do not extend appeal deadlines unless specifically granted
- Appellate courts may remand for Rule 60 consideration
- Strategic timing decisions affect both district court and appellate options

Settlement Leverage

Strong Rule 60 motions can:

- Reopen settlement discussions
- Demonstrate serious judgment enforcement problems
- Create cost pressures for judgment creditors
- Provide additional negotiating time and options

Common Examination Issues

Ground Selection

Students must distinguish between different Rule 60(b) grounds and their requirements:

- Understanding timing differences between subsections
- Recognizing when multiple grounds may apply
- Analyzing fact patterns for strongest relief theory
- Balancing finality concerns against equity considerations

Timing Calculations

Exam questions frequently test:

- One-year deadline calculations from judgment entry
- Reasonable time standards for unlimited grounds
- Interaction with appeal deadlines and other post-judgment motions
- Effect of discovery timing on motion filing requirements

RULE 61. HARMLESS ERROR

Rule 61 codifies the harmless error doctrine, preventing reversal of judgments unless errors affect substantial rights of parties.

Core Requirements

Substantial Rights Standard

Courts must disregard errors and defects that do not affect substantial rights of parties. This includes:

- Technical procedural violations without prejudicial impact
- Evidence rulings that do not affect trial outcomes
- Instruction errors that do not mislead juries
- Discovery violations with minimal case impact

Burden Allocation

Parties seeking relief based on claimed errors must demonstrate:

- Error occurrence during proceedings
- Prejudicial impact on substantial rights

- Connection between error and adverse outcome
- Lack of adequate alternative remedies

Application Principles

Error Categories

Different error types receive varying treatment:

a) Constitutional Errors: May require reversal despite minimal prejudice
b) Evidentiary Errors: Analyzed for impact on jury decision-making
c) Procedural Errors: Evaluated based on fairness and substantial rights
d) Instruction Errors: Assessed for misleading effect on verdict

Cumulative Impact

Courts consider:

- Individual errors that seem harmless in isolation
- Combined effect of multiple minor errors
- Overall fairness of proceedings despite technical violations
- Whether errors created systematic prejudice

Strategic Applications

Error Preservation

Effective appellate strategy requires:

- Timely objection to preserve error claims
- Clear record development of prejudicial impact
- Strategic focus on errors affecting substantial rights
- Documentation of cumulative error effects

Trial Court Discretion

Rule 61 supports trial court discretion by:

- Preventing reversal for technical violations
- Encouraging substance-focused judicial decisions
- Reducing appellate interference with trial management
- Promoting efficient case resolution

Practical Impact

Settlement Considerations

Rule 61's harmless error standard affects:

- Case valuation for settlement purposes
- Appeal likelihood assessments
- Cost-benefit analysis for continued litigation
- Leverage in post-trial negotiations

Judicial Efficiency

The harmless error doctrine promotes:

- Focus on substantial justice rather than technical compliance
- Reduced appellate reversals for minor violations

- Encouragement of practical trial court management
- Prevention of costly retrials for harmless errors

RULE 62. STAY OF PROCEEDINGS TO ENFORCE A JUDGMENT

Rule 62 governs when judgments may be enforced immediately and when execution must be stayed pending appeal or other proceedings.

Core Requirements

Automatic Stay Period (Rule 62(a))

Enforcement of money judgments is automatically stayed for 30 days after entry, providing time for post-judgment motions and appeal preparation.

Post-Judgment Motion Stays (Rule 62(b))

Filing certain post-judgment motions extends the automatic stay:

- Rule 50 motions for judgment as a matter of law
- Rule 52 motions for amended findings
- Rule 59 motions for new trial or amended judgment
- Stay continues until court disposes of motions

Injunction Standards (Rule 62(c))

Courts may grant stays of enforcement during appeal upon finding:

- Likelihood of success on appeal merits
- Irreparable harm without stay
- Balance of hardships favoring appellant
- Public interest considerations

Security Requirements (Rule 62(d))

Bond or Security

Courts may require appellant to post:

- Security for damages resulting from delayed enforcement
- Bond amounts sufficient to protect appellee interests
- Alternative security forms when cash bonds are impractical
- Modified security based on appellant's financial condition

Security Exceptions

Certain appellants may obtain stays without security:

- United States and its agencies
- State governments in some circumstances
- Indigent appellants meeting specific criteria
- Cases where security would be meaningless or impractical

Special Situations

Injunctive Relief (Rule 62(e))

Stays of injunctive relief require heightened scrutiny:

- Courts balance harm to both parties from stay or denial
- Public interest considerations often weigh heavily]
- Emergency circumstances may justify expedited review
- Constitutional issues may affect stay analysis

Class Action Considerations

Stays in class action contexts consider:

- Impact on absent class members
- Settlement distribution timing
- Administrative efficiency concerns
- Appellate review likelihood and timing

Strategic Applications

Appeal Planning

Rule 62 stays facilitate appellate strategy by:

- Providing time to prepare comprehensive appeals
- Preventing irreversible enforcement actions
- Maintaining status quo during appeal periods
- Enabling settlement discussions pending appeal

Enforcement Timing

- Judgment creditors must balance:
- Immediate enforcement advantages

- Appeal likelihood and probable success
- Debtor's asset preservation and location
- Collection efficiency during appeal periods

Practical Considerations

Bond Calculation

Courts consider various factors in setting bond amounts:

- Judgment size and potential interest accumulation
- Appellant's financial capacity
- Appellee's need for security
- Likelihood of successful appeal

Emergency Procedures

Some situations require expedited stay consideration:

- Imminent asset dissipation or transfer
- Time-sensitive business operations
- Constitutional rights implications
- Public health or safety concerns

RULE 63. JUDGE'S INABILITY TO PROCEED

Rule 63 addresses situations where judges become unable to continue with cases, providing mechanisms for case completion by successor judges.

Core Requirements

Substitution Authority

When judges become unable to proceed due to death, illness, or other circumstances, successor judges may:

- Complete proceedings if they determine they can do so fairly
- Consider the extent of previous proceedings
- Evaluate their ability to assess prior evidence and testimony
- Order new proceedings when necessary for fairness

Discretionary Standard

Successor judges have broad discretion to:

- Continue cases based on existing records
- Order partial retrials of specific issues
- Require complete new trials when appropriate
- Consider efficiency and fairness in making substitution decisions

Practical Applications

Common Situations

Rule 63 frequently applies when:

- Judges retire or transfer during pending litigation
- Illness prevents judges from continuing cases
- Recusal becomes necessary after partial proceedings
- Administrative reassignments affect case continuity

Case Assessment Factors

Successor judges typically consider:

- Complexity of proceedings to date
- Availability and quality of trial transcripts
- Amount of testimony and evidence presented
- Credibility determinations made by previous judge
- Time and cost implications of starting over

Strategic Considerations

Timing of Substitution

The stage of proceedings affects substitution decisions:

- Pre-trial: New judges can usually proceed without difficulty
- Mid-trial: Substitution often requires starting over due to credibility and witness assessment needs
- Post-trial: New judges may complete cases based on records when no additional factual determinations are needed
- Settlement Conferences: May need to be restarted with new judge involvement

Party Rights and Concerns

Parties affected by judicial substitution may:

- Request new trials when substitution occurs mid-proceeding

- Challenge successor judge's ability to assess prior evidence fairly
- Seek expedited scheduling to minimize delay impacts
- Negotiate settlements to avoid uncertainties from judicial changes

Efficiency Considerations

Administrative Impact

Rule 63 substitutions affect:

- Court docket management and scheduling
- Case completion timelines and delay
- Judicial resource allocation
- Settlement timing and leverage

Cost Implications

Judicial substitution may create:

- Additional attorney preparation time
- Witness re-testimony expenses
- Extended litigation timelines
- Settlement pressure from uncertainty

Title VIII - Provisional and Final Remedies

Title VIII provides the enforcement mechanisms for federal civil litigation, covering how courts secure assets, enforce judgments, and provide both temporary and permanent relief. These eight rules (Rules 64-71) bridge the gap between obtaining favorable judgments and actually collecting on them. The rules address everything from prejudgment asset seizure to final judgment enforcement, including the critical areas of injunctive relief and offers of judgment. Understanding these provisions is essential for practitioners who need to protect client interests during litigation and ensure that favorable outcomes translate into practical relief.

RULE 64. SEIZING A PERSON OR PROPERTY

Rule 64 incorporates state law remedies for securing persons or property to ensure availability for judgment satisfaction, providing federal courts with access to traditional state remedies while maintaining constitutional protections.

Core Requirements

State Law Integration

Rule 64 adopts the remedies available under the law of the state where the district court sits, creating a comprehensive framework that includes:

a) Attachment: Pre-judgment seizure of defendant property to secure potential judgments. Requirements typically include sworn affidavits showing debt existence, defendant's inability to pay, or risk of asset concealment.
b) Garnishment: Seizure of property held by third parties, commonly wages or bank accounts. Garnishment procedures vary significantly among states, with different notice requirements and exemption protections.
c) Replevin: Recovery of specific personal property wrongfully detained by defendants. Requires showing superior right to possession and posting security for potential damages.
d) Sequestration: Court custody of disputed property pending litigation resolution. Particularly useful when multiple parties claim ownership of specific assets.
e) Ne Exeat: Prevention of defendant departure from jurisdiction, though rarely used given constitutional travel right concerns.

Constitutional Limitations

All Rule 64 procedures must comply with due process requirements established in cases like Sniadach v. Family Finance Corp. and Goldberg v. Kelly:

a) Notice Requirements: Defendants generally entitled to notice before seizure except in extraordinary circumstances involving immediate danger of asset dissipation.

b) Hearing Rights: Post-seizure hearings must be available promptly, with burden on seizure applicants to justify continued restraint.

c) Specificity Standards: Applications must identify particular property and provide factual basis for seizure necessity.

Practical Applications

Asset Investigation

Effective Rule 64 practice requires thorough asset investigation before seizure attempts:

- Bank account identification through subpoenas and depositions
- Real estate record searches in relevant jurisdictions
- Business interest discovery through corporate filings
- Personal property location through surveillance and investigation

Timing Considerations

Rule 64 remedies are most effective when applied strategically:

- Early case filing to establish jurisdiction for seizure procedures
- Coordination with complaint service to prevent advance warning

- Consideration of defendant's likely response and counter-strategies
- Integration with settlement discussions and case development

Multi-State Complications

When defendants have assets in multiple states, practitioners must coordinate:

- Different state law requirements for similar remedies
- Jurisdictional issues for out-of-state property seizure
- Full Faith and Credit enforcement of seizure orders
- Cost-benefit analysis of multi-jurisdictional proceedings

Strategic Considerations

Risk Assessment

Rule 64 applications require careful evaluation of:

- Likelihood of ultimate success on underlying claims
- Defendant's actual asset holdings and location
- Potential wrongful seizure liability and bond requirements
- Effect on ongoing business relationships and settlement prospects

Security Requirements

Most state procedures require bonds or other security to protect defendants from wrongful seizure:

- Bond amounts typically related to property value or potential damages
- Security may be reduced for strong cases or increased for questionable claims
- Alternative security forms may be available for indigent plaintiffs
- Government entities often exempted from security requirements

Common Pitfalls

Procedural Compliance Failures

Frequent errors include:

- Insufficient factual support in seizure applications
- Failure to comply with state-specific notice and hearing requirements
- Inadequate property identification in seizure orders
- Misunderstanding of exemption protections under applicable state law

Strategic Overreach

Common tactical mistakes involve:

- Excessive seizure requests that appear punitive rather than protective
- Failure to consider settlement impact of aggressive asset seizure
- Inadequate investigation leading to fruitless seizure attempts

- Ignoring constitutional limitations in emergency seizure situations

RULE 65. INJUNCTIONS AND RESTRAINING ORDERS

Rule 65 governs the most powerful provisional remedies available to federal courts: temporary restraining orders and preliminary injunctions that can preserve rights and prevent irreparable harm during litigation.

Core Requirements

Temporary Restraining Orders (Rule 65(b))

Ex Parte Standards

Courts may grant TROs without notice only when:

- Specific facts clearly show immediate and irreparable injury will result before opposing party can be heard
- Applicant's attorney certifies efforts made to notify opposing parties or states reasons why notice should not be required
- Moving party provides security for costs and damages incurred by wrongfully restrained parties

Content Requirements

Every TRO must:

- State date and hour of issuance

- Define precisely the injury and state why it is irreparable
- State why order was granted without notice if applicable
- Set specific expiration time not exceeding 14 days unless extended for good cause
- Be promptly filed in clerk's office and entered in record

Service and Notice

TROs must be served immediately on opposing parties with copies of motion papers and supporting documents. Personal service is preferred but alternative methods may be authorized when necessary.

Preliminary Injunctions (Rule 65(a))

Four-Factor Test

Courts evaluate preliminary injunction requests using established criteria:

a) Likelihood of Success on Merits: Probability that moving party will ultimately prevail in litigation. Courts require substantial likelihood, not mere possibility of success.
b) Irreparable Harm: Injury that cannot be adequately compensated by monetary damages. Must be imminent and certain, not speculative or remote.
c) Balance of Hardships: Comparative harm to parties from granting or denying injunctive relief. Courts weigh inconvenience, financial impact, and practical consequences.

d) Public Interest: Effect of injunctive relief on broader community interests, regulatory policies, and societal values.

Evidentiary Standards

Preliminary injunction hearings require substantial factual development:

- Live testimony often preferred over affidavit evidence
- Cross-examination rights for opposing parties
- Documentary evidence with proper authentication
- Expert testimony when technical issues are involved

Security Requirements (Rule 65(c))

Courts may require security for payment of costs and damages incurred by wrongfully enjoined parties. Security amount is discretionary and may be nominal when:

- Moving party has limited financial resources
- Case presents strong likelihood of success
- Opposing party unlikely to suffer significant damages
- Government entities seek injunctive relief

Types of Injunctive Relief

Prohibitory Injunctions

Orders preventing specific conduct or activities:

- Non-compete agreement enforcement
- Trade secret protection orders
- Environmental compliance requirements

- Contract breach prevention

Mandatory Injunctions

Orders requiring affirmative conduct, held to higher standards due to greater intrusion:

- Specific performance of contractual obligations
- Restoration of previous conditions
- Compliance with regulatory requirements
- Disclosure of confidential information

Status Quo Orders

Preservation of existing conditions pending litigation resolution:

- Employment relationship maintenance
- Business operation continuation
- Asset preservation and management
- Customer relationship protection

Substantive Law Applications

Intellectual Property

Injunctive relief is common in IP litigation:

- Patent infringement cases require clear validity and infringement showing
- Trademark disputes focus on likelihood of confusion and market harm
- Copyright cases emphasize irreparable harm from continued infringement

- Trade secret protection often justifies emergency relief

Employment Law

Workplace injunctions address various issues:

- Non-compete enforcement requires reasonable scope and legitimate interests
- Trade secret protection during employee transition periods
- Wrongful termination cases may seek reinstatement relief
- Union activity and labor dispute management

Commercial Litigation

Business disputes frequently involve injunctive relief:

- Contract performance and breach prevention
- Partnership and joint venture disputes
- Supplier and distributor relationship conflicts
- Competitive practice and unfair competition claims

Strategic Applications

Timing and Presentation

Successful injunctive relief requires:

- Prompt application after discovering need for relief
- Comprehensive factual record development
- Clear legal theory connecting facts to applicable standards
- Practical proposed order terms that are enforceable

Settlement Leverage

Injunctive relief motions often influence case resolution:

- Strong motions create pressure for favorable settlements
- Emergency hearings provide early judicial assessment of case merits
- Cost and inconvenience of compliance may motivate resolution
- Preservation of business relationships through negotiated solutions

Case Management Impact

Preliminary injunction practice affects entire case development:

- Accelerated discovery to support motion practice
- Early expert witness retention and preparation
- Compressed briefing schedules requiring immediate attention
- Judicial case management and scheduling considerations

Common Examination Issues

Standard Application

Law school exams frequently test:

- Proper application of four-factor preliminary injunction test

- Understanding of irreparable harm requirements and examples
- Balance of hardships analysis in specific factual contexts
- Integration of substantive law with procedural standards

Emergency Procedures

Students must understand:

- Ex parte TRO requirements and limitations
- Notice and hearing rights in emergency situations
- Security and bond requirements for various party types
- Appeal rights and standards for injunctive relief orders

RULE 65.1. PROCEEDINGS AGAINST A SECURITY PROVIDER

Core Requirements

Rule 65.1 establishes procedures for enforcing security posted under Rule 65 or other court orders. When parties post bonds or other security for injunctive relief, opposing parties may proceed directly against security providers using the same procedures applicable to original defendants.

Direct Action Rights

Injured parties may sue security providers without first obtaining judgment against principal obligors, streamlining enforcement and ensuring meaningful protection.

Procedural Integration

Rule 65.1 proceedings follow standard civil procedure rules for service, pleading, discovery, and trial, ensuring comprehensive protection for all parties.

Practical Applications

This rule ensures that security requirements under Rule 65 provide meaningful protection rather than illusory promises, encouraging responsible bonding and insurance practices in injunctive relief contexts.

1. Surety Bond Enforcement: Commercial sureties face direct liability for wrongful injunction damages, creating incentives for careful risk assessment and bond pricing.
2. Alternative Security Forms: Courts may accept various security types including cash deposits, letters of credit, and real estate liens, with Rule 65.1 enforcement applying to all forms.

RULE 66. RECEIVERS

Rule 66 incorporates traditional equity practice for appointing receivers to manage property during litigation, providing courts with flexible tools for complex property disputes and business management situations.

Core Requirements

Appointment Standards

Courts consider multiple factors when evaluating receiver appointments:

- Necessity for property preservation or management
- Inadequacy of alternative remedies
- Consent or agreement of interested parties
- Qualifications and impartiality of proposed receivers
- Cost and practical feasibility of receivership management

Types of Receiverships

Different receivership forms serve various purposes:

a) Custodial Receivers: Preserve and maintain property pending dispute resolution without active management responsibilities.
b) Operating Receivers: Manage ongoing businesses including daily operations, employee relations, and strategic decisions.
c) Liquidating Receivers: Sell assets and distribute proceeds according to court orders and legal priorities.
d) Equity Receivers: Address complex multi-party disputes with competing claims requiring judicial supervision.

Powers and Duties

Management Authority

Receivers typically possess broad powers including:

- Asset control and management
- Contract negotiation and performance
- Employee hiring and termination
- Litigation conduct on behalf of receivership estates
- Financial reporting and accounting to courts

Fiduciary Obligations

Receivers owe duties to:

- Courts appointing them
- All parties with interests in receivership property
- Creditors and other stakeholders
- General public when receiverships involve public utilities or services

Compensation Structure

Receiver compensation requires court approval and typically involves:

- Reasonable hourly rates for professional services
- Percentage-based fees for asset sales or recoveries
- Reimbursement for reasonable expenses and professional fees
- Performance incentives for successful business operations or asset recovery

Strategic Applications

Business Dispute Resolution

Receiverships provide solutions for:

- Deadlocked partnerships or joint ventures
- Corporate management disputes with competing factions
- Family business conflicts requiring neutral management
- Dissolution proceedings requiring asset preservation

Asset Recovery

Receivers serve important functions in:

- Fraud and embezzlement cases requiring asset tracing
- Ponzi scheme and investment fraud recoveries
- Professional malpractice cases with ongoing business operations
- Environmental cleanup and liability management

Practical Considerations

Cost-Benefit Analysis

Receivership involves significant expenses:

- Receiver fees and professional costs
- Administrative overhead and reporting requirements
- Potential business disruption and value diminution
- Extended litigation and resolution timelines

Alternative Remedies

Courts prefer less drastic solutions when available:

- Temporary injunctions preserving specific assets
- Appointment of neutral managers or advisors
- Mediation or arbitration of underlying disputes
- Negotiated management agreements between parties

RULE 67. DEPOSIT INTO COURT

Rule 67 allows parties to deposit disputed funds or property with courts when multiple claimants exist or when liability is clear but proper recipients are uncertain, providing efficient resolution mechanisms for stakeholder disputes.

Core Requirements

Deposit Authority

Courts may order or permit deposits when:

- Multiple parties claim ownership of specific funds or property
- Stakeholders face potential multiple liability exposure
- Uncertainty exists regarding proper payment recipients
- Parties agree to judicial resolution of ownership disputes

Investment and Management

Courts establish procedures for:

- Safe investment of deposited funds in interest-bearing accounts
- Periodic reporting on deposit status and earnings

- Distribution authorization upon dispute resolution
- Administrative fee assessment for deposit management

Integration with Interpleader

Rule 22 Coordination

Rule 67 deposits often accompany interpleader actions:

- Stakeholders deposit disputed funds while claimants litigate ownership
- Courts may require deposits as condition of interpleader relief
- Investment earnings may be allocated among claimants or stakeholders
- Distribution occurs according to final judgments or settlement agreements

Strategic Benefits

Deposit practice provides advantages including:

- Protection from multiple liability exposure
- Interest earnings preservation during litigation
- Simplified distribution procedures after resolution
- Reduced administrative burdens for stakeholders

Practical Applications

Insurance Disputes

Rule 67 commonly applies when:

- Policy limits are insufficient for multiple claims
- Coverage disputes exist between insurers and insureds
- Multiple insurers dispute coverage allocation
- Settlement funds require court approval for distribution

Estate and Trust Matters

Fiduciary disputes may involve deposits when:

- Will contests affect distribution rights
- Trust interpretation disputes arise among beneficiaries
- Executor or trustee powers are challenged
- Tax obligations create uncertainty about net distributions

Commercial Contexts

Business disputes may require deposits for:

- Construction project funds with lien claimants
- Escrow disputes in real estate transactions
- Partnership dissolution and asset distribution
- Contract performance bonds and security deposits

RULE 68. OFFER OF JUDGMENT

Rule 68 creates incentives for reasonable settlement by shifting certain costs when plaintiffs reject defendants' settlement offers and fail to obtain better results at trial, promoting efficient case resolution and reducing litigation expenses.

Core Requirements

Offer Procedures

Rule 68 offers must satisfy specific requirements:

- Service at least 14 days before trial commencement
- Specific terms including all damages, costs, and attorney fees if applicable
- Written form with clear acceptance deadline
- Service on all parties when multiple plaintiffs exist

Acceptance and Rejection

Formal procedures govern offer responses:

- Written acceptance required within 14 days of service
- Automatic withdrawal if not accepted within deadline
- Entry of judgment according to offer terms upon acceptance
- No judicial approval required for standard offer acceptance

Cost Shifting Mechanism

When plaintiffs obtain judgments less favorable than rejected offers:

- Plaintiffs become liable for defendants' costs incurred after offer service
- "Costs" include most litigation expenses but typically exclude attorney fees
- Burden on defendants to document post-offer costs with reasonable specificity

- Courts have discretion to determine reasonableness of claimed costs

Cost Categories

Recoverable Costs

Post-offer costs typically include:

- Court filing fees and administrative charges
- Deposition costs including court reporter fees
- Witness fees and travel expenses
- Document copying and exhibit preparation
- Expert witness fees within statutory limits
- Process service and subpoena costs

Non-Recoverable Items

Courts generally exclude:

- Attorney fees unless authorized by separate statute or contract
- Internal administrative and overhead expenses
- Travel and accommodation costs for attorneys
- Investigative and preparation expenses
- Settlement negotiation costs

Strategic Applications

Defendants' Perspective

Effective Rule 68 practice requires:

- Careful timing to maximize settlement pressure
- Realistic offer amounts based on case assessment
- Comprehensive cost documentation after offer rejection
- Integration with summary judgment and other dispositive motion practice

Offer Calculation Strategy

Successful offers typically:

- Reflect realistic case valuation including damages and cost exposure
- Consider plaintiff's litigation funding and cost sensitivity
- Account for trial uncertainty and jury unpredictability
- Include attorney fees when authorized by applicable law

Multiple Defendant Situations

Complex cases may involve:

- Coordinated offers from multiple defendants
- Allocation of cost responsibility among defendants
- Individual versus joint offer strategies
- Settlement coordination to avoid inconsistent results

Plaintiffs' Considerations

Evaluation Factors

Rule 68 offers require careful analysis of:

- Probability of obtaining better results at trial

- Litigation costs likely to be incurred through trial completion
- Defendant's ability to document and recover post-offer costs
- Time value of money and litigation expense considerations

Risk Assessment

Plaintiff attorneys must evaluate:

- Strength of liability and damages evidence
- Jury appeal and case presentation effectiveness
- Defendant's litigation budget and cost documentation capabilities
- Appeal likelihood and additional cost exposure

Client Counseling

Effective representation requires explaining:

- Cost-shifting consequences of offer rejection
- Risk-benefit analysis for continued litigation
- Settlement alternatives and negotiation possibilities
- Financial implications of various outcome scenarios

Common Pitfalls

Offer Drafting Errors

Frequent mistakes include:

- Ambiguous terms creating enforcement problems

- Failure to specify all relief components including costs and fees
- Inadequate service documentation
- Timing errors affecting offer validity

Cost Documentation Failures

Defendants often struggle with:

- Inadequate record keeping for post-offer expenses
- Failure to distinguish recoverable from non-recoverable costs
- Insufficient supporting documentation for claimed expenses
- Delay in presenting cost recovery motions

RULE 69. EXECUTION

Rule 69 incorporates state law procedures for enforcing money judgments through execution against debtor assets, providing comprehensive collection mechanisms while respecting debtor protection rights under applicable state law.

Core Requirements

State Law Integration

Federal courts apply execution procedures available in the state where the district court sits, creating comprehensive enforcement framework including:

a) Writ of Execution: Court orders directing sheriffs to seize and sell debtor property to satisfy judgments.
b) Personal Property Execution: Seizure of moveable assets including vehicles, equipment, inventory, and household goods subject to exemption protections.
c) Real Estate Execution: Forced sale of land and buildings through judicial sale procedures with redemption rights and homestead protections.
d) Wage Garnishment: Ongoing seizure of employment income subject to federal and state limitations protecting subsistence needs.
e) Bank Account Garnishment: Seizure of deposit accounts with notice procedures and exemption protections for certain fund types.

Discovery in Aid of Execution

Rule 69 authorizes comprehensive post-judgment discovery to locate debtor assets:

- Depositions of judgment debtors and third parties
- Document production regarding financial condition
- Asset disclosure requirements under oath
- Investigation of transfers and concealment attempts

Exemption Protections

State law exemptions limit execution scope:

- Homestead exemptions protecting primary residences
- Personal property exemptions for essential items
- Wage garnishment limitations based on income levels
- Retirement account and insurance protections

- Tools of trade and professional equipment exemptions

Practical Applications

Asset Investigation Strategy

Effective execution requires systematic investigation:

- Public record searches for real estate ownership
- Business entity searches for corporate interests and partnerships
- Financial institution discovery through subpoenas and depositions
- Vehicle and personal property location through various databases
- Employment and income source identification

Execution Timing Considerations

Strategic execution practice involves:

- Prompt action after judgment entry to prevent asset dissipation
- Coordination with appeal timing and stay considerations
- Seasonal and business cycle factors affecting asset availability
- Integration with settlement discussions and payment plan negotiations

Multi-State Enforcement

Interstate execution requires:

- Registration of foreign judgments in states where assets are located
- Understanding of different state exemption and procedural laws
- Coordination of multiple enforcement actions
- Cost-benefit analysis for multi-jurisdictional collection efforts

Strategic Applications

Pre-Judgment Planning

Successful collection often requires early preparation:

- Asset discovery during litigation through standard discovery procedures
- Preservation of collection rights through settlement agreement drafting
- Understanding of debtor's business operations and cash flow cycles
- Identification of collection alternatives including guarantors and security interests

Collection Priority

Effective execution strategy prioritizes:

- Liquid assets providing immediate collection potential
- Income sources enabling ongoing recovery through garnishment
- Business assets that may appreciate or generate revenue

- Real estate providing long-term collection security despite slower realization

Debtor Cooperation Incentives

Strategic collection may involve:

- Payment plan negotiations providing predictable income streams
- Partial settlements reducing overall judgment amounts
- Cooperation agreements providing asset disclosure in exchange for execution delays
- Workout arrangements preserving debtor business operations while ensuring payment

Common Challenges

Asset Protection Schemes

Sophisticated debtors may employ:

- Fraudulent transfers to family members or related entities
- Domestic or international trust structures
- Business entity manipulation to shield personal assets
- Geographic asset distribution to complicate enforcement

Exemption Planning

Debtors may legitimately use:

- Homestead planning to protect residential real estate

- Retirement account maximization to shield funds from creditors
- Insurance and annuity products with creditor protection features
- Business structure optimization to separate personal and business assets

RULE 70. ENFORCING A JUDGMENT FOR A SPECIFIC ACT

Rule 70 provides enforcement mechanisms when judgments require defendants to perform specific acts other than paying money, including court-appointed performance and contempt proceedings for willful violation.

Core Requirements

Performance Alternatives

When defendants fail to comply with specific performance judgments, courts may:

- Direct that acts be performed by court-appointed persons at judgment debtor expense
- Issue writs of assistance authorizing third parties to perform required acts
- Employ contempt proceedings to compel compliance through coercive measures
- Fashion alternative relief achieving substantially similar results

Contempt Proceedings

Willful violation of specific performance orders may result in:

- Civil contempt with coercive imprisonment or fines
- Criminal contempt punishment for past violations
- Remedial sanctions including attorney fees and costs
- Alternative performance mechanisms reducing future compliance problems

Common Applications

Real Estate Conveyances

Courts frequently enforce:

- Specific performance of purchase and sale agreements
- Deed execution and property transfer requirements
- Easement creation and boundary adjustment orders
- Lease execution and occupancy agreements

Business and Commercial Orders

Specific performance may involve:

- Intellectual property assignments and transfers
- Non-compete agreement compliance
- Partnership agreement performance
- Corporate governance and management directives

Document Production

Courts may order:

- Execution of documents required by contract or regulation
- Corporate record production and authentication
- Financial disclosure and reporting compliance
- Regulatory filing and submission requirements

Strategic Considerations

Enforcement Practicality

Successful specific performance requires:

- Clear and definite order terms that can be objectively measured
- Practical feasibility of performance by defendant or third parties
- Adequate supervision and monitoring mechanisms
- Cost-effective alternatives when direct performance is impossible

Contempt Strategy

Effective contempt practice involves:

- Clear documentation of order violation and willful non-compliance
- Exhaustion of alternative enforcement mechanisms
- Proportionate sanctions related to violation severity
- Remedial rather than purely punitive relief focus

Alternative Relief

When specific performance proves impractical:

- Monetary damages as substitute relief
- Third-party performance at defendant expense
- Modified performance requirements addressing practical obstacles
- Creative relief fashioned to achieve judgment purposes

Practical Challenges

Performance Impossibility

Courts must address:

- Changed circumstances making performance impossible
- Third-party rights conflicting with performance requirements
- Regulatory or legal obstacles preventing compliance
- Cost and feasibility considerations for alternative performance

International Complications

Cross-border enforcement may involve:

- Foreign law restrictions on specific performance
- Diplomatic and treaty considerations
- Alternative jurisdiction options for enforcement
- Practical limitations on court authority and process service

RULE 71. ENFORCING RELIEF FOR OR AGAINST A NONPARTY

Rule 71 addresses enforcement situations where judgment relief affects persons not parties to the original action, ensuring that judgments remain effective despite changed circumstances or third-party involvement.

Core Requirements

Nonparty Categories

Rule 71 applies to various nonparty situations:

- Transferees of judgment debtor property after judgment entry
- Successors in interest to original parties through merger, acquisition, or inheritance
- Third parties holding debtor assets as agents, trustees, or custodians
- Entities controlled by judgment debtors through ownership or management

Due Process Requirements

Enforcement against nonparties requires:

- Adequate notice of proposed enforcement action
- Opportunity to be heard regarding enforcement propriety
- Clear showing of nonparty relationship to original judgment

- Procedural safeguards protecting nonparty rights and interests

Supplemental Jurisdiction

Courts may exercise supplemental jurisdiction over nonparty enforcement proceedings when:

- Claims arise from same transaction or occurrence as original judgment
- Enforcement is necessary to provide complete relief
- Nonparty involvement is integral to judgment effectiveness
- Federal and state law policies support extended jurisdiction

Practical Applications

Asset Transfer Situations

Rule 71 commonly applies when:

- Judgment debtors transfer assets to family members or related entities
- Business reorganization affects asset ownership and control
- Corporate mergers or acquisitions change entity structure
- Estate administration requires enforcement against personal representatives

Successor Liability

Courts may enforce judgments against:

- Corporate successors through merger or asset acquisition
- Partnership successors following dissolution and reformation
- Trust beneficiaries when trustees are judgment debtors
- Family members receiving fraudulent transfers

Third-Party Asset Control

Enforcement may reach:

- Banks and financial institutions holding debtor accounts
- Business partners with joint control over partnership assets
- Agents and representatives with authority over debtor property
- Custodians and trustees managing assets for debtor benefit

Strategic Considerations

Investigation Requirements

Effective nonparty enforcement requires:

- Comprehensive asset tracing to identify current ownership
- Corporate and business relationship analysis
- Documentation of transfer timing and circumstances

- Evidence of control relationships and beneficial ownership

Procedural Planning

Successful nonparty enforcement involves:

- Proper service of process and pleading requirements
- Joinder of necessary parties to avoid multiple proceedings
- Coordination with main case enforcement efforts
- Settlement consideration with both debtors and nonparties

Legal Theory Development

Enforcement theories may include:

- Fraudulent transfer law providing recovery from transferees
- Successor liability doctrines in corporate and partnership contexts
- Agency and trust law creating third-party obligations
- Piercing corporate veil and alter ego theories

Common Challenges

Procedural Complexity

Nonparty enforcement often involves:

- Multiple court proceedings in different jurisdictions
- Complex notice and service requirements
- Coordination with ongoing collection efforts

- Integration with bankruptcy and other insolvency proceedings

Legal Limitations

Courts must respect:

- Nonparty due process rights and procedural protections
- Statute of limitations on fraudulent transfer and successor liability claims
- Good faith purchaser protections under applicable law
- Constitutional limitations on court jurisdiction and authority

TITLE IX - SPECIAL PROCEEDINGS

Title IX addresses specialized procedures that fall outside the standard litigation framework, covering condemnation proceedings and the expanded role of magistrate judges in federal civil practice. These three rules (Rules 71.1-73) establish distinct procedural frameworks for unique situations requiring judicial attention. Rule 71.1 governs eminent domain proceedings where government entities acquire private property for public use, while Rules 72-73 define magistrate judges' authority in pretrial management and trial by consent. Understanding these provisions is essential for practitioners handling government litigation, complex case management, and efficient judicial resource allocation in modern federal practice.

RULE 71.1. CONDEMNING REAL OR PERSONAL PROPERTY

Rule 71.1 establishes comprehensive procedures for federal condemnation proceedings, providing government entities with streamlined mechanisms for acquiring private property while protecting property owners' constitutional rights through due process safeguards.

Core Requirements

Scope and Application

Rule 71.1 applies to federal condemnation actions where government entities exercise eminent domain power to acquire private property for public use. The rule governs both real estate and personal property acquisition, including:

a) Direct Federal Condemnation: Cases where federal agencies directly condemn property for federal projects such as military installations, federal buildings, national parks, or interstate highway systems.
b) Federally Funded Projects: State and local government condemnation proceedings that receive federal funding and must comply with federal procedural requirements.
c) Cross-Border Acquisitions: Multi-state projects requiring coordinated condemnation proceedings in multiple federal districts.

Constitutional Foundation

All Rule 71.1 proceedings must satisfy Fifth Amendment requirements:

- Public use requirement for legitimate governmental purposes
- Just compensation obligation providing fair market value
- Due process protections ensuring adequate notice and hearing opportunities
- Equal protection considerations preventing discriminatory taking practices

Pleading Requirements

Complaint Elements (Rule 71.1(c))

Condemnation complaints must include specific information:

a) Governmental Authority: Citation to statutory or constitutional authority empowering the condemning entity to exercise eminent domain power.
b) Public Use Declaration: Clear statement of public purpose justifying property acquisition, with sufficient detail to demonstrate legitimate governmental interest.
c) Property Description: Precise identification of property to be condemned, including legal descriptions, addresses, and survey information sufficient for accurate identification.
d) Property Interest Description: Specific identification of property interests sought, whether fee simple, easements, leaseways, or other partial interests.
e) Owner Identification: Names and addresses of all known property owners, lienholders, and other parties with interests in condemned property.

Service Requirements

Rule 71.1 establishes special service procedures:

- Personal service preferred for all identified property owners
- Publication service authorized for unknown owners or parties whose addresses cannot be determined with reasonable diligence
- Posted notice on condemned property when practical and appropriate

- Service on governmental entities holding liens or other interests

Compensation Procedures

Deposit Requirements (Rule 71.1(j))

Condemning authorities must typically deposit estimated compensation with the court:

- Amount based on governmental appraisal of property value
- Immediate availability for property owner withdrawal
- Interest accumulation during proceeding pendency
- Additional deposits when initial estimates prove inadequate

Appraisal and Valuation

Compensation determination involves comprehensive valuation process:

- Professional appraisal by qualified experts considering highest and best use
- Comparable sales analysis in relevant market areas
- Special consideration for unique properties without ready comparables
- Separate valuation of improvements, fixtures, and business operations

Compensation Standards

Just compensation requires fair market value determination:

- Value at time of taking rather than complaint filing date
- Consideration of property's highest and best use potential
- Exclusion of value increases attributable to condemned project itself
- Include severance damages when partial taking affects remaining property value

Procedural Mechanisms

Possession Procedures (Rule 71.1(k))

Courts may authorize immediate possession upon:

- Deposit of estimated compensation with court
- Notice to property owners and opportunity for hearing
- Finding that immediate possession serves important public interest
- Adequate protection for property owners through compensation and appeal rights

Discovery and Evidence

Condemnation cases involve specialized discovery:

- Property inspection rights for both parties
- Expert witness testimony on valuation issues
- Documentary evidence including sales records, tax assessments, and development plans
- Site visits and jury view procedures when appropriate

Trial Procedures

Compensation trials follow modified procedures:

- Right to jury trial on compensation issues
- Specialized jury instructions on valuation standards
- Expert witness testimony on complex valuation issues
- Court supervision of damage assessment and award calculation

Strategic Applications

Government Perspective

Effective condemnation practice requires:

- Thorough pre-filing property investigation and title examination
- Comprehensive appraisal and valuation documentation
- Strategic timing to minimize property value appreciation
- Coordination with project planning and construction schedules

Property Owner Defense

Successful defense strategies include:

- Independent appraisal challenging governmental valuations
- Highest and best use analysis maximizing compensation potential
- Severance damage claims for partial takings

- Constitutional challenges to public use determinations

Settlement Considerations

Many condemnation cases resolve through negotiation:

- Early settlement discussions before formal proceedings
- Mediation and alternative dispute resolution
- Partial settlements on uncontested valuation issues
- Structured payment arrangements for large compensation awards

Special Situations

Partial Takings

When government acquires only part of larger properties:

- Separate valuation of taken portion and remaining property
- Severance damage calculations for diminished remaining value
- Access and utility easement considerations
- Future development impact on remaining property

Business Relocation

Commercial property condemnation may involve:

- Business interruption and relocation expense compensation
- Goodwill and going concern value consideration
- Employee displacement and retraining costs
- Equipment moving and setup expenses

Historic and Special Properties

Unique properties require special consideration:

- Historic preservation law compliance
- Cultural and community value assessments
- Replacement cost analysis for irreplaceable properties
- Environmental impact and mitigation requirements

Common Pitfalls

Inadequate Property Investigation

Frequent errors include:

- Incomplete title examination missing important interests
- Insufficient property boundary and survey verification
- Failure to identify all parties with compensable interests
- Inadequate environmental and regulatory compliance review

Valuation Disputes

Common compensation problems involve:

- Unrealistic governmental appraisals leading to extended litigation
- Failure to consider special property characteristics and uses
- Inadequate comparable sales analysis in unique market areas

- Insufficient severance damage analysis for partial takings

RULE 72. MAGISTRATE JUDGES; PRETRIAL ORDER

Rule 72 defines magistrate judges' authority to handle pretrial matters in civil cases, establishing the framework for judicial efficiency through delegated case management while preserving district judges' ultimate authority over dispositive issues.

Core Requirements

Magistrate Judge Authority

Rule 72 establishes two categories of magistrate judge authority with different review standards:

Non-Dispositive Matters (Rule 72(a))

Magistrate judges may hear and determine pretrial matters that do not dispose of claims or defenses, including:

- Discovery disputes and motion practice
- Scheduling conferences and case management orders
- Pre-trial conferences and settlement discussions
- Evidence rulings and motion in limine determinations
- Temporary restraining order applications
- Prisoner civil rights case screening and management

Review Standard: District judges may modify or set aside magistrate judge orders on non-dispositive matters only if they are "clearly erroneous or contrary to law."

Dispositive Motions (Rule 72(b))

Magistrate judges may only make recommendations on dispositive matters, including:

- Summary judgment motions
- Motions to dismiss under Rule 12(b)(6)
- Motions for judgment on the pleadings
- Habeas corpus petitions
- Motions to suppress evidence in criminal cases
- Social Security disability appeals

Review Standard: District judges must conduct de novo review of objected-to portions of magistrate judge recommendations on dispositive matters.

Referral Mechanisms

Automatic Referrals

Many districts establish automatic referral systems for certain case types:

- Prisoner civil rights litigation requiring extensive case management
- Social Security disability appeals with standardized review procedures
- Discovery-intensive commercial litigation needing active management

- Pro se cases requiring additional judicial attention and guidance

Discretionary Referrals

District judges may refer specific matters based on:

- Case complexity requiring specialized attention
- Judicial calendar and resource allocation needs
- Parties' consent to magistrate judge handling
- Efficiency considerations for repetitive or routine matters

Objection and Review Procedures

Objection Requirements (Rule 72(b)(2))

Parties seeking district judge review of magistrate judge recommendations must:

- File written objections within 14 days of service
- Specify objected-to portions with reasonable detail
- Provide legal and factual basis for disagreement
- Serve objections on all parties

Waiver Consequences

Failure to file timely objections may result in:

- Waiver of appellate review rights
- Adoption of magistrate judge recommendations without further analysis
- Limitation of subsequent appeal grounds
- Procedural default affecting case resolution

De Novo Review Standards

District judges must independently review:

- Legal conclusions and rule applications
- Factual findings disputed in objections
- Mixed questions of law and fact
- Constitutional and statutory interpretation issues

Strategic Applications

Case Management Efficiency

Effective magistrate judge utilization provides:

- Accelerated discovery resolution and case progression
- Specialized expertise in complex procedural issues
- Consistent case management across similar litigation types
- Reduced burden on district judge calendars

Settlement and Alternative Dispute Resolution

Magistrate judges often facilitate:

- Settlement conferences with neutral judicial perspective
- Mediation and arbitration referral decisions
- Creative resolution mechanisms for complex disputes
- Pre-trial conferences focusing on case narrowing and efficiency

Discovery Management

Magistrate judge authority includes:

- Electronic discovery protocol establishment
- Discovery dispute resolution and sanction recommendations
- Protective order and confidentiality agreement approval
- Expert witness and deposition scheduling coordination

Practical Considerations

Strategic Forum Selection

Litigants may consider magistrate judge assignment when:

- Cases require extensive pretrial management and discovery oversight
- Specialized expertise in particular legal areas provides advantages
- Settlement prospects benefit from neutral judicial facilitation
- Calendar timing and efficiency concerns outweigh other factors

Objection Strategy

Effective objection practice requires:

- Careful analysis of magistrate judge recommendations
- Strategic decision-making about which issues warrant district judge review

- Comprehensive briefing on objected-to legal and factual conclusions
- Consideration of appellate review preservation needs

RULE 73. MAGISTRATE JUDGES; TRIAL BY CONSENT; APPEAL

Rule 73 authorizes magistrate judges to conduct jury and non-jury trials with parties' consent, providing full judicial authority equivalent to district judges while establishing direct appeal routes to courts of appeals.

Core Requirements

Consent Requirements (Rule 73(a))

Magistrate judge trial authority requires:

- Written consent from all parties
- Voluntary agreement without coercion or pressure
- Understanding that magistrate judges possess full trial authority
- Knowledge of direct appeal rights to courts of appeals

Consent Process

Courts must ensure informed consent through:

- Clear explanation of magistrate judge trial authority and qualifications
- Notice that consent is voluntary and may be withdrawn before trial commencement

- Information about appeal procedures and standards for magistrate judge trials
- Opportunity for parties to consult with counsel before consent decisions

Trial Authority (Rule 73(b))

Consenting parties vest magistrate judges with complete trial authority including:

- Jury selection and trial management
- Evidence ruling and legal standard application
- Final judgment entry with full legal effect
- Post-trial motion determination and relief

Appeal Procedures (Rule 73(c))

Direct Appeal Rights

Appeals from magistrate judge trials go directly to courts of appeals, bypassing district judge review:

- Same appellate standards as district judge trial appeals
- No intermediate district judge review or approval required
- Full appellate jurisdiction over legal and factual determinations
- Standard appellate briefing and argument procedures

Appeal Standards

Courts of appeals review magistrate judge trials using identical standards applied to district judge trials:

- De novo review of legal conclusions
- Clear error standard for factual findings
- Abuse of discretion review for evidentiary and procedural rulings
- Harmless error analysis for trial errors

Strategic Applications

Efficiency Advantages

Magistrate judge trials often provide:

- Earlier trial dates due to less congested calendars
- Streamlined case management and pretrial procedures
- Consistent judicial attention throughout case progression
- Reduced continuance and scheduling complications

Settlement Facilitation

Magistrate judge involvement may enhance settlement prospects through:

- Early neutral evaluation of case strengths and weaknesses
- Ongoing judicial involvement in settlement discussions
- Creative resolution mechanisms and alternative dispute approaches
- Reduced formality encouraging open communication

Specialized Expertise

Some magistrate judges possess particular expertise valuable for specific case types:

- Intellectual property and technology litigation experience
- Employment law and discrimination case familiarity
- Complex commercial dispute management skills
- Pro se litigant assistance and case management experience

Consent Considerations

Timing Decisions

Parties should evaluate magistrate judge consent based on:

- Calendar availability and trial scheduling preferences
- Case complexity and judicial expertise requirements
- Settlement prospects and alternative resolution potential
- Appeal likelihood and strategic timing considerations

Withdrawal Rights

Consent may be withdrawn:

- Before reference to magistrate judge becomes effective
- For good cause shown with court approval
- When circumstances change affecting consent appropriateness

- Subject to case management and scheduling impact considerations

Practical Benefits

Resource Allocation

Magistrate judge trials serve judicial system efficiency by:

- Reducing district judge trial calendar pressure
- Providing specialized case management for routine litigation types
- Enabling district judge focus on complex or novel legal issues
- Supporting overall federal court productivity and case resolution

Quality Considerations

Many magistrate judges bring valuable experience including:

- Extensive trial practice before judicial appointment
- Specialized training in case management and alternative dispute resolution
- Focus on efficiency and practical case resolution
- Accessibility and communication skills enhancing litigant satisfaction

Common Applications

Case Type Suitability

Magistrate judge trials work particularly well for:

- Commercial disputes with straightforward legal issues
- Employment discrimination cases requiring factual development
- Contract and tort litigation with clear damage calculations
- Intellectual property cases within magistrate judge expertise areas

Party Considerations

Consent decisions often depend on:

- Relationship between case complexity and available judicial expertise
- Calendar timing and business needs for prompt resolution
- Settlement prospects and alternative dispute resolution preferences
- Cost considerations and litigation budget constraints

Title X - District Courts and Clerks

Title X addresses the administrative machinery that keeps federal litigation functioning smoothly. While these rules may seem mundane compared to the dramatic motions practice of earlier titles, they govern essential courthouse operations that affect every case. Understanding these provisions helps practitioners navigate court systems efficiently and avoid procedural missteps that can derail otherwise strong cases. These rules establish how courts conduct business, maintain records, and issue orders that bind parties and guide litigation progress.

RULE 77. CONDUCTING BUSINESS; CLERK'S AUTHORITY; NOTICE OF AN ORDER OR JUDGMENT

Rule 77 governs how district courts conduct regular business and establishes the clerk's authority in case administration.

Core Requirements

Rule 77 establishes the fundamental framework for district court operations, defining when and how courts conduct business while delineating the significant authority vested in court clerks.

Court Sessions (Rule 77(a))

District courts may conduct business at any time, but judges often establish regular hours and procedures for routine matters. Courts need not hold formal sessions for all business, allowing flexibility in case management.

Clerk's Authority (Rule 77(b))

The court clerk holds substantial independent authority including:

- Entering default judgments when liability and damages are certain
- Issuing writs and processes necessary for court orders
- Acting on unopposed motions for extensions of time
- Performing ministerial acts that implement court decisions

Notice Requirements (Rule 77(d))

Service of notice for judgments and orders follows specific requirements:

- Parties must receive immediate notice of entry of judgment or appealable orders
- Notice may be provided by mail, electronic means, or other court-approved methods
- The notice requirement protects appellate rights by starting appeal periods

Practical Applications

1. Clerk's Office Strategy: Experienced practitioners develop working relationships with clerk's office staff, who often provide valuable guidance on local practices and procedural requirements. Clerks can resolve routine issues without judicial intervention, saving time and costs.
2. Default Judgment Efficiency: Rule 77(b) allows clerks to enter defaults in straightforward cases, streamlining resolution when defendants fail to respond and damages are easily calculable.
3. Appeal Timing Protection: Proper notice under Rule 77(d) ensures that appeal periods begin running correctly, protecting parties' appellate rights while providing certainty about when judgments become final.

Strategic Considerations

1. Local Practice Variations: Different districts implement Rule 77 differently, particularly regarding clerk authority and notice procedures. Practitioners must learn local customs and standing orders that supplement Rule 77's basic framework.
2. Electronic Notice Systems: Most courts now provide electronic notice to registered users, but practitioners must ensure their contact information remains current to receive timely notice of court actions.
3. Emergency Situations: Understanding clerk authority helps in emergency situations where immediate action

is needed outside regular court hours or when judges are unavailable.

RULE 78. HEARING MOTIONS; SUBMISSION ON BRIEFS

"By rule or order, the court may provide for submitting motions on briefs, without oral hearings."

Core Requirements

Rule 78 gives courts broad discretion in determining how to handle motion practice, balancing efficiency against the traditional right to oral argument.

Discretionary Nature

Courts have complete discretion to decide which motions require hearings and which may be submitted on written briefs alone. This flexibility allows courts to manage heavy dockets while ensuring adequate consideration of important issues.

Written Submission Standard

Many routine motions are now decided "on the papers" without oral hearings. Courts typically reserve hearings for complex issues, cases involving credibility determinations, or matters where oral argument would substantially aid decision making.

Local Rule Implementation

Districts often adopt local rules specifying which types of motions are routinely heard without oral argument and establishing procedures for requesting hearings when desired.

Practical Applications

1. Motion Practice Efficiency: The trend toward written submission has accelerated motion practice, with many routine discovery disputes, extension requests, and procedural motions resolved quickly without hearings.
2. Hearing Request Strategy: When practitioners believe oral argument would be helpful, they should explicitly request hearings in their motion papers and explain why oral argument would assist the court.
3. Brief Quality Importance: With fewer oral hearings, written briefs carry greater weight in motion practice. Clear, concise, and persuasive writing becomes more crucial when courts decide motions solely on submitted papers.

Strategic Considerations

1. Local Practice Research: Practitioners must research local practices regarding motion hearings, as customs vary significantly between districts and even among judges within districts.
2. Hearing Requests: Strategic decisions about when to request hearings depend on case complexity,

relationship strength with opposing counsel, and the particular judge's preferences.

3. Settlement Conference Opportunities: Some courts use motion hearings as informal settlement conferences, creating opportunities for resolution that written submissions cannot provide.

RULE 79. RECORDS KEPT BY THE CLERK

Rule 79 requires the clerk to keep specific records and makes them available for public inspection.

Core Requirements

Rule 79 establishes essential record keeping requirements that create the official case record and provide public access to court proceedings.

Civil Docket (Rule 79(a))

The clerk must maintain a civil docket showing:

- All papers filed in each case
- Process issued and returns made
- Appearances and withdrawals of attorneys
- Orders, verdicts, and judgments entered
- Jury compositions and verdicts

Public Access

Court records remain open for public inspection except when sealed by court order or protected by specific statutes. This transparency principle ensures public oversight of judicial proceedings.

Record Preservation

Clerks must preserve court records according to federal retention schedules, ensuring availability for appeals, post-judgment proceedings, and historical research.

Practical Applications

1. Case Research: The civil docket provides comprehensive case histories useful for understanding procedural postures, identifying patterns in particular judges' rulings, and researching opponent counsel's litigation strategies.
2. Appeal Preparation: Accurate docket maintenance is crucial for appeals, as appellate courts rely on district court records to understand procedural history and identify appealable orders.
3. Public Relations Considerations: Public access to court records means sensitive information may become publicly available unless properly sealed, requiring strategic thinking about confidentiality protection.

Strategic Considerations

1. Docket Monitoring: Practitioners benefit from regularly monitoring case dockets, both in their own cases and in related litigation, to stay informed about procedural developments and judicial rulings.

2. Sealing Motions: When cases involve sensitive commercial information or personal data, practitioners should consider sealing motions to protect confidential material from public disclosure.
3. Electronic Access: Most federal courts now provide online docket access through PACER, enabling real-time case monitoring and research capabilities.

RULE 80. STENOGRAPHIC TRANSCRIPT AS EVIDENCE

"If stenographically reported testimony at a hearing or trial is admissible in evidence at a later trial, the testimony may be proved by a transcript certified by the person who reported it."

Core Requirements

Rule 80 addresses the use of previous testimony in subsequent proceedings, establishing authentication requirements for stenographic transcripts.

Certification Requirement

Transcripts must be certified by the court reporter who created the original stenographic record. This certification authenticates the accuracy and completeness of the testimony reproduction.

Admissibility Standards

The rule assumes that properly certified transcripts are admissible when the underlying testimony would be admissible, but does not address the separate question of when previous testimony may be used as evidence.

Integration with Evidence Rules

Rule 80 works in conjunction with Federal Rules of Evidence governing the admissibility of former testimony, particularly Rule 804(b)(1) regarding testimony of unavailable witnesses.

Practical Applications

1. Deposition Use: While Rule 80 specifically addresses trial testimony, similar principles apply to using deposition transcripts in subsequent proceedings.
2. Appeal Preparation: Certified transcripts are essential for appeals involving disputes about trial proceedings, testimony content, or judicial rulings.
3. Related Case Strategy: In cases involving similar parties or issues, previous certified testimony may provide valuable evidence or strategic intelligence.

Strategic Considerations

1. Court Reporter Relationships: Maintaining positive relationships with court reporters facilitates obtaining timely, accurate transcripts for appeals and other proceedings.
2. Transcript Timing: Ordering daily copy during important trials ensures immediate availability of certified transcripts for post-trial motions and appeals.

3. Cost Management: Transcript costs can be substantial in lengthy trials, requiring budgeting considerations and strategic decisions about which portions to order.

Integration with Other Rules

1. Rule 32 Connection: Rule 80 complements Rule 32's provisions for using depositions, creating a comprehensive framework for utilizing previous testimony in litigation.
2. Appeal Rule Coordination: Rule 80 supports Federal Rule of Appellate Procedure 10's requirements for assembling appellate records including trial transcripts.
3. Evidence Rule Interaction: Rule 80's authentication provisions work with Federal Rules of Evidence to provide a complete framework for using previous testimony as evidence.

Common Examination Issues

1. Authentication Requirements: Students must understand the difference between transcript certification under Rule 80 and the admissibility standards for former testimony under evidence rules.
2. Practical Application: Exam questions often test understanding of when and how previous testimony may be used in subsequent proceedings.
3. Integration Analysis: Complex exam problems may require analyzing Rule 80 in conjunction with discovery rules, evidence rules, and appellate requirements.

Title XI - General Provisions

Title XI serves as the Federal Rules' capstone, addressing fundamental questions about when, where, and how the rules apply. These provisions resolve jurisdictional gaps, coordinate with other court systems, and establish judicial authority over local practice. While practitioners may not cite these rules daily, they provide essential framework principles that govern rule interpretation and application across the federal system. Understanding Title XI prevents costly mistakes in removed actions, multijurisdictional litigation, and cases involving specialized proceedings that fall outside standard civil practice.

RULE 81. APPLICABILITY OF THE RULES IN GENERAL; REMOVED ACTIONS

Rule 81 defines the scope of Federal Rules application and addresses special situations where standard procedures may not apply.

Core Requirements

Rule 81 establishes which proceedings are governed by the Federal Rules and provides special procedures for cases that enter federal court through unusual paths or involve hybrid legal proceedings.

General Applicability (Rule 81(a))

The Federal Rules apply to all civil actions in district courts, with specific exceptions outlined in subsections. This broad coverage ensures uniform procedure across the federal system while recognizing that some specialized proceedings require different approaches.

Removed Actions (Rule 81(c))

When state court cases are removed to federal court, specific timing adjustments apply:

- Defendants who have not answered in state court get the full time allowed by Rule 12 to respond
- Time runs from receiving notice of removal or service of summons, whichever is later
- State court proceedings remain valid up to the removal point
- Federal procedure governs all subsequent proceedings

Proceedings Excluded or Modified

Rule 81 identifies proceedings where Federal Rules apply differently or not at all, including:

- Criminal proceedings (governed by Federal Rules of Criminal Procedure)
- Bankruptcy proceedings (governed by Federal Rules of Bankruptcy Procedure)
- Certain admiralty proceedings (supplemented by Admiralty Rules)
- Administrative proceedings and judicial review of agency actions

Removed Actions Practice

1. Timing Calculations: Removal creates complex timing issues that practitioners must navigate carefully. Defendants who answered in state court cannot raise Rule 12(b) defenses in federal court unless they were preserved under state law. However, defendants who had not answered get fresh opportunities to raise federal defenses.
2. Jurisdictional Considerations: Removal invokes federal question or diversity jurisdiction, but the case must have been properly filed in state court initially. Federal courts cannot cure jurisdictional defects through removal.
3. Discovery Coordination: State court discovery remains valid after removal, but federal discovery rules govern future proceedings. Courts may need to address conflicts between state and federal discovery standards.

Practical Applications

1. Removal Strategy: Defense counsel must carefully evaluate whether removal benefits their client, considering differences between state and federal procedure, jury pools, judges, and substantive law applications.
2. Plaintiff Response: Plaintiffs may seek remand for lack of jurisdiction or procedural defects in removal. Understanding removal requirements helps identify grounds for remand motions.

3. Case Management: Removed cases often require special attention to procedural transitions, discovery coordination, and scheduling adjustments to accommodate the change in forum.

Strategic Considerations

1. Forum Shopping Defense: Removal serves as defendants' primary tool for countering plaintiff forum shopping, moving cases from potentially unfavorable state courts to federal forum.
2. Timing Pressures: The 30-day removal deadline creates urgency in evaluating removal options and gathering necessary documentation for removal petitions.
3. Cost-Benefit Analysis: Removal involves immediate costs and may complicate proceedings, requiring careful evaluation of strategic benefits against practical drawbacks.

RULE 82. JURISDICTION AND VENUE UNAFFECTED

"These rules do not extend or limit the jurisdiction of the district courts or the venue of actions in those courts."

Core Requirements

Rule 82 establishes a crucial limitation on Federal Rules interpretation, ensuring that procedural rules cannot expand or contract federal court authority beyond constitutional and statutory boundaries.

Jurisdictional Neutrality

The Federal Rules are procedural tools that operate within existing jurisdictional limits but cannot create new bases for federal court authority. Subject matter jurisdiction must derive from constitutional and statutory sources, not procedural rules.

Venue Protection

Similarly, the rules cannot override venue statutes or create new venue options beyond those established by Congress. Rule 82 prevents procedural rules from effectively expanding geographic reach of federal courts.

Separation of Powers

Rule 82 reflects separation of powers principles by ensuring that judicial rulemaking does not encroach on legislative authority over court jurisdiction and venue.

Practical Applications

1. Jurisdictional Analysis: Practitioners must analyze subject matter jurisdiction independently of Federal Rules provisions. Rules like supplemental jurisdiction concepts in joinder cannot create jurisdiction where none exists statutorily.
2. Venue Challenges: Rule 82 confirms that improper venue challenges proceed under venue statutes (28

U.S.C. §§ 1391-1412) rather than Federal Rules provisions.

3. Limitation of Procedural Innovation: Courts cannot use Federal Rules creatively to solve jurisdictional or venue problems that require legislative solutions.

Strategic Considerations

1. Jurisdictional Planning: Case planning must begin with careful jurisdictional and venue analysis independent of procedural strategies under Federal Rules.
2. Rule Interpretation: When Federal Rules provisions might be read to affect jurisdiction or venue, Rule 82 counsels narrow interpretation that preserves legislative prerogatives.
3. Appeal Considerations: Jurisdictional and venue challenges often involve different appellate standards and timing than procedural rule disputes.

RULE 83. RULES BY DISTRICT COURTS; JUDGE'S DIRECTIVES

Rule 83 authorizes district courts to adopt local rules and individual judges to issue case management directives.

Core Requirements

Rule 83 establishes the hierarchical relationship between Federal Rules, local rules, and individual judicial directives while ensuring that local variations serve legitimate case management purposes without undermining system uniformity.

Local Rules Authority (Rule 83(a))

District courts may adopt local rules governing practice, provided they:

- Are consistent with Federal Rules and federal statutes
- Do not duplicate Federal Rules provisions
- Are adopted only after public notice and opportunity for comment
- Are designed to address genuine local needs or conditions

Individual Judge Directives (Rule 83(b))

Individual judges may regulate practice in their courtrooms through standing orders or case-specific directives, subject to consistency requirements with Federal Rules and local rules.

Publication and Notice

Local rules must be published and readily available to practitioners. Many districts now maintain comprehensive websites with local rules, forms, and judicial preferences.

Practical Applications

1. Local Practice Research: Effective practice requires thorough knowledge of local rules and judicial preferences in each district where attorneys practice.

Local rules often address practical details not covered by Federal Rules.

2. Compliance Challenges: Practitioners must ensure compliance with Federal Rules, local rules, and individual judicial directives, creating complex regulatory environments in some districts.
3. Strategic Advantages: Understanding local practices provides competitive advantages through more efficient case management, better judge relationships, and avoided procedural pitfalls.

Local Rule Categories

1. Case Management: Many local rules address scheduling, discovery management, and motion practice procedures that supplement Federal Rules requirements.
2. Technology Integration: Local rules increasingly address electronic filing, video conferencing, and digital evidence presentation requirements.
3. Specialized Proceedings: Districts may adopt local rules for patent cases, class actions, or other specialized litigation types that require modified procedures.

Strategic Considerations

1. Multi-District Practice: Attorneys practicing in multiple districts must maintain current knowledge of varying local requirements and adapt strategies accordingly.

2. Relationship Building: Understanding and following local practices helps build positive relationships with court personnel and judges.

3. Efficient Practice: Local rule compliance reduces delays, sanctions risks, and client costs while improving case outcomes.

RULE 85. TITLE

"These rules may be cited as the Federal Rules of Civil Procedure."

Core Requirements

Rule 85 provides the official title for citation purposes, ensuring uniform reference to the Federal Rules across legal documents and judicial opinions.

Citation Consistency

The official title promotes consistent citation practices in briefs, judicial opinions, and legal scholarship, reducing confusion and supporting clear legal communication.

Professional Standards

Proper citation demonstrates professional competence and attention to detail, while incorrect citations may undermine credibility.

Integration with Citation Systems

The official title integrates with established citation systems like the Bluebook and ALWD Citation Manual.

Practical Applications

1. Document Preparation: All legal documents should use proper Federal Rules citations, typically abbreviated as "Fed. R. Civ. P." in formal documents.
2. Legal Research: Consistent citation practices facilitate legal research and case law analysis by creating uniform reference standards.
3. Professional Communication: Proper citation enhances professional communication between attorneys, courts, and legal scholars.

RULE 86. EFFECTIVE DATES

Rule 86 addresses when rule amendments take effect and their application to pending cases.

Core Requirements

Rule 86 manages the transition between different versions of Federal Rules, ensuring fair application of procedural changes while maintaining legal certainty.

Amendment Process:

Rule amendments follow the process established by the Rules Enabling Act (28 U.S.C. § 2072), typically taking effect December 1 following Congressional approval periods.

Retroactivity Principles

Rule amendments generally apply to pending cases unless retroactive application would cause injustice or unfairness to parties who relied on previous rules.

Transition Management

Courts must determine which rule version applies to specific procedural steps in cases spanning rule amendments.

Practical Applications

1. Pending Case Analysis: When rule amendments occur during litigation, practitioners must analyze which procedural steps are governed by old versus new rules.
2. Strategic Timing: Understanding effective dates may influence timing of filings, motions, or other procedural steps to take advantage of favorable rule versions.
3. Compliance Planning: Law firms must update forms, procedures, and training materials to reflect rule amendments while managing transition periods.

Strategic Considerations

1. Rule Monitoring: Practitioners should monitor proposed rule amendments through the judicial

conference process to anticipate changes affecting their practice areas.
2. Client Communication: Rule changes may affect case strategies, timelines, or costs, requiring client communication about procedural developments.
3. System Updates: Technology systems, forms, and office procedures require updates to reflect rule amendments.

RULE 87. CIVIL RULES EMERGENCY

Rule 87 addresses emergency rule modifications during national emergencies or disasters.

Core Requirements

Rule 87 provides authority for emergency modifications to Federal Rules when extraordinary circumstances prevent normal court operations or create unfair procedural burdens.

Emergency Authority

The Chief Justice may authorize emergency modifications to Federal Rules during declared national emergencies or when extraordinary circumstances affect court operations.

Limited Scope

Emergency modifications must address specific problems created by the emergency situation and cannot make permanent changes to Federal Rules.

Temporary Duration

Emergency rule modifications automatically expire unless extended, ensuring that emergency measures do not become permanent without proper rulemaking processes.

Practical Applications

1. Pandemic Response: Rule 87 provided authority for COVID-19 related modifications including extended deadlines, remote proceedings, and modified service requirements.
2. Disaster Management: Natural disasters, terrorist attacks, or other emergencies may trigger Rule 87 modifications to ensure continued court access and fair proceedings.
3. Technology Integration: Emergency situations may accelerate adoption of technology solutions that later influence permanent rule amendments.

Strategic Considerations

1. Monitoring Requirements: Practitioners must stay informed about emergency modifications that may affect pending cases or procedural requirements.
2. Adaptation Planning: Law firms should develop contingency plans for emergency situations that may disrupt normal court operations or procedural requirements.

3. Client Service: Emergency modifications may create opportunities to serve clients better through extended deadlines or alternative procedures.

Integration with Emergency Authorities

1. Administrative Authority: Rule 87 works with administrative authorities of individual courts to address emergency situations comprehensively.
2. Constitutional Limits: Emergency modifications remain subject to constitutional requirements for due process and access to courts.
3. Legislative Coordination: Emergency rule modifications coordinate with legislative emergency authorities to ensure comprehensive response to extraordinary situations.

Common Examination Issues

1. Rule Application: Students must understand which proceedings are governed by Federal Rules versus other procedural systems.
2. Removal Timing: Complex removal scenarios frequently appear on examinations, testing understanding of timing rules and procedural transitions.
3. Local Rule Authority: Questions may test understanding of the relationship between Federal Rules, local rules, and judicial directives.
4. Amendment Application: Exam problems may involve rule changes during pending litigation, requiring

analysis of which rule version applies to specific procedural steps.

TITLE XII- APPENDIX OF FORMS [ABROGATED]

The Federal Rules of Civil Procedure originally included an Appendix of Forms (Title XII) containing 82 standardized form pleadings, motions, and other court documents. These forms served as official templates from the rules' inception in 1938 through December 1, 2015, when they were formally abrogated by the Supreme Court. The abrogation reflects the legal profession's evolution toward more sophisticated pleading practices and the forms' increasing obsolescence in modern litigation. While practitioners once relied heavily on these standardized templates, contemporary legal practice demands more tailored, fact-specific pleadings that address the complexity of today's cases and judicial expectations.

HISTORICAL CONTEXT AND PURPOSE

Original Function

The Appendix of Forms was designed to provide practical guidance for implementing the Federal Rules' "notice pleading" standard established in Rule 8. The forms demonstrated how to satisfy pleading requirements with simple, straightforward language that gave fair notice of claims and defenses without requiring detailed factual allegations.

Key Categories Included:

- Summons forms for various defendant types
- Complaint templates for common causes of action
- Answer formats and affirmative defenses
- Motion templates for standard procedural requests
- Discovery forms and notices
- Judgment and execution documents

Illustrative Nature

Rule 84 (also abrogated) explicitly stated that forms in the appendix were "sufficient under these rules." This provision gave the forms quasi-authoritative status, meaning pleadings substantially following the forms were legally adequate even if stylistically simple.

Safe Harbor Protection: Attorneys using forms substantially similar to the appendix forms were protected from Rule 11 sanctions or motions to dismiss for failure to state a claim, provided the underlying facts supported the legal theory.

REASONS FOR ABROGATION

Outdated Content

By 2015, many forms reflected legal standards and practices that had evolved significantly since their original drafting. Changes in substantive law, particularly in areas like employment discrimination and civil rights, made some forms inadequate for contemporary practice.

Specific Problems:

- Employment law forms failed to reflect current Title VII and ADA requirements
- Civil rights forms did not incorporate § 1983 jurisprudential developments
- Contract and tort forms were too simplistic for complex commercial litigation
- Discovery forms predated electronic discovery requirements

Misleading Guidance

The Advisory Committee found that practitioners sometimes relied too heavily on the forms without adapting them to specific factual circumstances or evolving legal standards. This mechanical application led to inadequate pleadings that failed to meet courts' heightened expectations following Twombly and Iqbal.

Judicial Evolution: Federal courts increasingly expected more detailed, fact-specific pleadings that demonstrated plausible claims for relief, making the forms' bare-bones approach potentially insufficient.

Maintenance Burden

Keeping 82 forms current with changing law, procedure, and practice proved administratively burdensome. The Advisory Committee concluded that resources were better devoted to refining the rules themselves rather than maintaining parallel form guidance.

PRACTICAL IMPLICATIONS POST-ABROGATION

Pleading Standards Unchanged

The abrogation did not alter substantive pleading requirements under Rules 8, 9, and 12. Notice pleading remains the standard, and complaints must still provide fair notice of claims and grounds for relief.

Continuing Validity: Pleadings that would have satisfied requirements using the old forms generally continue to meet Rule 8 standards, though practitioners must ensure compliance with current legal requirements independent of the forms.

Alternative Resources

Practitioners now rely on various alternative sources for pleading guidance:

a) Commercial Form Books: Publishers like West, Lexis, and American Jurisprudence maintain comprehensive form collections updated regularly for current law.
b) Local Practice Guides: Many federal districts and bar associations publish local form collections reflecting regional practice preferences and judicial expectations.
c) Court Websites: Individual courts increasingly provide forms for common motions and standard procedures on their websites.
d) Bar Organization Resources: State and specialty bar associations maintain form libraries for member use.

Strategic Considerations

The abrogation reflects the profession's movement toward more individualized, strategic pleading practices:

1. Tailored Approach: Modern practice emphasizes crafting pleadings specifically adapted to case facts, applicable law, and forum preferences rather than using standardized templates.
2. Factual Development: Contemporary pleadings typically include more factual detail to satisfy Twombly/Iqbal plausibility standards while avoiding unnecessary admissions.
3. Defensive Considerations: Without safe harbor protection from standardized forms, practitioners must more carefully evaluate pleading choices for strategic implications.

CURRENT STATUS AND RECOMMENDATIONS

Along with the forms themselves, Rule 84 was abrogated, eliminating the explicit "sufficiency" protection that forms provided. This change requires practitioners to independently verify that their pleadings satisfy all applicable legal and procedural requirements.

Best Practices for Practitioners

1. Independent Verification: Attorneys must ensure pleadings comply with current substantive law, procedural requirements, and local rules without relying on potentially outdated form language.

2. Factual Specificity: Include sufficient factual allegations to satisfy plausibility standards while avoiding unnecessary detail that might limit litigation flexibility.
3. Local Adaptation: Research local court preferences, standing orders, and judicial expectations that may affect pleading effectiveness beyond basic rule compliance.
4. Regular Updates: Maintain current awareness of legal developments affecting common causes of action and adjust pleading practices accordingly.

Examination and Bar Preparation

For law students and bar candidates, the abrogation means:

1. Focus on Rules: Emphasis should be placed on understanding the underlying rules rather than memorizing specific form language.
2. Principle Application: Develop skills in applying pleading principles to varied factual situations rather than relying on template approaches.
3. Current Awareness: Stay informed about recent developments in pleading standards and judicial expectations in relevant jurisdictions.

The abrogation of Title XII represents the profession's maturation from reliance on standardized templates toward more sophisticated, individualized advocacy practices that better serve clients in contemporary legal environments.

TITLE XIII - SUPPLEMENTAL RULES FOR ADMIRALTY OR MARITIME CLAIMS AND ASSET FORFEITURE ACTIONS

The Supplemental Rules for Admiralty or Maritime Claims and Asset Forfeiture Actions represent a specialized body of federal procedure governing maritime law disputes and government asset forfeiture cases. These rules supplement, rather than replace, the Federal Rules of Civil Procedure, addressing unique procedural requirements that arise from the distinctive nature of admiralty jurisdiction and maritime commerce. Originally focused solely on admiralty practice, these rules were expanded in 2006 to include civil asset forfeiture procedures, reflecting the government's increased reliance on forfeiture actions in law enforcement. Understanding these supplemental rules is essential for practitioners handling maritime disputes, vessel arrests, limitation of liability proceedings, and federal forfeiture cases.

RULE A. GENERAL PROVISIONS

Scope and Application

Rule A establishes the foundational framework for supplemental rule application, defining when these specialized procedures apply and how they interact with the standard Federal Rules.

Admiralty Jurisdiction Requirements

- Case must involve maritime subject matter under 28 U.S.C. § 1333
- Federal court must have admiralty or maritime jurisdiction
- Traditional civil procedure applies unless supplemental rules specify otherwise
- Local admiralty rules may provide additional requirements

Integration with Federal Rules

The supplemental rules operate alongside, not in place of, the Federal Rules of Civil Procedure. When conflicts arise, the supplemental rules control for admiralty and forfeiture matters, while the Federal Rules govern general procedural questions not addressed by the supplemental rules.

Local Rule Authority

Federal district courts with significant admiralty caseloads often adopt local admiralty rules addressing practical concerns like vessel custody, security requirements, and motion practice. These local rules must be consistent with the supplemental rules but may provide additional detail for routine procedures.

Practical Application

1. Pleading Requirements: Admiralty complaints must identify the basis for admiralty jurisdiction and specify whether the action is in rem, quasi in rem, or in

personam. This jurisdictional foundation determines which supplemental rules apply.

2. Notice Requirements: Maritime cases often involve multiple potentially interested parties (vessel owners, cargo interests, insurers, crew members) requiring broader notice than typical civil litigation.

RULE B. IN PERSONAM ACTIONS; ATTACHMENT AND GARNISHMENT

Attachment Procedures

Rule B provides specialized attachment procedures for maritime cases where personal jurisdiction over defendants may be difficult to establish through conventional means.

Prerequisites for Attachment

- Defendant not found within the district
- Maritime claim that would justify attachment under admiralty law
- Plaintiff unable to obtain personal service on defendant
- Property belonging to defendant exists within the district

Attachment Process

a) Verified Complaint: Plaintiff must file a verified complaint stating facts supporting attachment and identifying specific property to be attached.

b) Security Requirement: Courts typically require plaintiff to post security for wrongful attachment, protecting defendant from damages if attachment proves unjustified.

c) Property Identification: Attachment orders must specifically describe property to be attached, whether tangible assets, bank accounts, or other interests within the district.

Strategic Considerations

1. Forum Selection: Rule B attachment provides a mechanism for establishing jurisdiction in favorable forums where defendants have attachable property but are not otherwise subject to personal jurisdiction.
2. Security Interests: Maritime liens and other security interests may complicate attachment proceedings, requiring careful analysis of priority rights among competing claimants.
3. International Implications: Rule B procedures frequently involve international defendants and foreign-flagged vessels, requiring attention to treaty obligations and international comity principles.

RULE C. IN REM ACTIONS; SPECIAL PROVISIONS

Foundation of In Rem Proceedings

Rule C governs actions against vessels, cargo, and other maritime property, reflecting admiralty law's unique ability to treat property as the defendant in legal proceedings.

In Rem Jurisdiction Requirements

- Valid maritime lien or other basis for proceeding against property
- Property must be within the district when action commences
- Proper arrest and custody procedures must be followed
- Constitutional due process requirements must be satisfied

Arrest Procedures

a) Warrant Application: Plaintiff must apply for warrant of arrest by verified complaint stating facts supporting the maritime claim and identifying the property with reasonable specificity.

b) Judicial Review: Magistrate judges or district judges review warrant applications, examining both the underlying maritime claim and procedural compliance.

c) Custody Arrangements: Upon arrest, property comes under court custody through U.S. Marshals, who arrange appropriate storage, maintenance, and security pending litigation resolution.

Notice Requirements

Rule C mandates extensive notice procedures to protect the rights of all interested parties:

1. Publication Notice: Notice of arrest must be published in approved newspapers and may require additional publication in maritime trade publications.

2. Direct Notice: When known parties have interests in the arrested property, direct service of process is required in addition to publication.
3. International Notice: Foreign-flagged vessels may require notice through diplomatic channels or under international agreements.

Practical Challenges

1. Custody Costs: Maintaining arrested vessels and cargo generates substantial daily expenses that must be addressed through security deposits or court-approved payment arrangements.
2. Emergency Situations: Rule C procedures must accommodate maritime emergencies where immediate action is necessary to preserve property or prevent environmental damage.
3. Multiple Claimants: Admiralty cases frequently involve multiple claimants asserting competing interests in the same property, requiring careful case management and priority determinations.

RULE D. POSSESSORY, PETITORY, AND PARTITION ACTIONS

Specialized Maritime Property Disputes

Rule D addresses unique forms of maritime property litigation that have no direct equivalent in common law procedure.

Possessory Actions

a) These actions determine immediate possession rights to vessels or maritime property without resolving underlying ownership questions.
b) Requirements: Plaintiff must show superior right to immediate possession based on charter parties, management agreements, or other contractual arrangements.
c) Temporary Relief: Courts may award temporary possession pending full adjudication when plaintiff demonstrates likely success and potential harm from continued adverse possession.

Petitory Actions

These proceedings determine ultimate ownership or title to maritime property, similar to quiet title actions in real property law.

a) Title Issues: Complex vessel ownership structures, including corporate arrangements, flags of convenience, and beneficial ownership concepts, frequently complicate petitory proceedings.
b) Evidence Requirements: Establishing maritime title often requires documentation from multiple jurisdictions, including flag state records, mortgage recordings, and international registration systems.

Partition Actions

When multiple parties own interests in maritime property, partition actions divide interests or force judicial sale with proceeds distribution.

a) Valuation Challenges: Maritime property valuation requires specialized expertise considering vessel condition, market conditions, and operational factors affecting value.

RULE E. ACTIONS IN REM AND QUASI IN REM; GENERAL PROVISIONS

Comprehensive In Rem Framework

Rule E provides detailed procedures applicable to all actions against maritime property, establishing uniform standards for arrest, custody, and disposition.

Security and Counter-Security

a) Plaintiff Security: Courts require security from plaintiffs to cover potential damages from wrongful arrest, including vessel operating costs and lost profits.
b) Release Security: Defendants may obtain property release by posting adequate security, typically a bond equal to the claim amount plus costs and interest.
c) Security Valuation: Determining appropriate security amounts requires consideration of claim values, property values, and potential additional costs during litigation pendency.

Custody and Preservation

1. Marshal Responsibilities: U.S. Marshals assume custody of arrested property and bear responsibility for its preservation and maintenance during litigation.
2. Maintenance Requirements: Vessels require ongoing maintenance, insurance, crew payments, and port charges, creating substantial ongoing obligations during arrest periods.
3. Sale Procedures: When custody costs threaten to exceed property value, courts may order judicial sales to preserve value for claimants.

Intervention and Claims

1. Claim Procedures: Interested parties must file claims within specified time limits to participate in in rem proceedings and protect their interests.
2. Intervention Rights: Rule 24 intervention principles apply, but admiralty practice recognizes broader intervention rights for parties with maritime interests.
3. Priority Determinations: Courts must resolve competing claims according to admiralty lien priority rules, which differ significantly from common law security interest priorities.

RULE F. LIMITATION OF LIABILITY

Statutory Foundation

Rule F implements procedures for limitation of liability actions under 46 U.S.C. § 30501 et seq., allowing vessel owners to limit liability to the vessel's post-casualty value.

Limitation Requirements

a) Timely Filing: Limitation actions must be commenced within six months of receiving written notice of claims exceeding vessel value.
b) Privity and Knowledge: Vessel owners must establish lack of privity and knowledge regarding the casualty causing damages.
c) Adequate Security: Owners must post security equal to vessel value plus pending freight to invoke limitation protection.

Concourse Proceedings

1. Claim Consolidation: Limitation actions create a concourse where all related claims are consolidated for adjudication in a single proceeding.
2. Injunctive Relief: Courts issue injunctions preventing prosecution of related claims in other forums while limitation proceedings are pending.
3. Claims Administration: The court supervises claims filing, evaluation, and distribution procedures similar to bankruptcy administration.

Strategic Considerations

1. Cost-Benefit Analysis: Limitation proceedings involve substantial costs and complexity, making economic analysis crucial for determining whether limitation is advantageous.
2. Insurance Coordination: Limitation actions must be coordinated with insurance coverage to avoid prejudicing coverage or creating conflicts between limitation and insurance strategies.
3. International Implications: International conventions may limit the availability or effectiveness of U.S. limitation proceedings for foreign casualties or foreign-flag vessels.

RULE G. FORFEITURE ACTIONS IN REM

Scope and Foundation

Rule G, added in 2006, establishes comprehensive procedures for civil forfeiture actions, creating a unified federal framework that applies to all statutory forfeiture proceedings.

1. Statutory Authority: Civil forfeiture actions must be grounded in specific statutory authority, commonly including drug forfeiture statutes (21 U.S.C. § 881), customs laws (19 U.S.C. § 1595a), money laundering statutes (18 U.S.C. § 981), and various regulatory forfeiture provisions.
2. Constitutional Requirements: Rule G procedures must satisfy constitutional due process requirements, incorporating Supreme Court precedents regarding

notice, hearing rights, and burden of proof standards in civil forfeiture cases.

3. Property Subject to Forfeiture: The rule covers forfeiture of real property, personal property, monetary instruments, and intangible assets connected to criminal activity or regulatory violations.

Complaint and Warrant Procedures

Verified Complaint Requirements

- Government must file verified complaint describing property with reasonable particularity
- Complaint must state statutory basis for forfeiture
- Facts supporting probable cause for forfeiture must be alleged
- Property location and custody arrangements must be addressed

Warrant for Arrest in Rem

Similar to admiralty arrest procedures, forfeiture actions require judicial approval for property seizure through warrant procedures that balance law enforcement needs with property owner rights.

a) Probable Cause Standard: Courts must find probable cause that property is subject to forfeiture before issuing arrest warrants, applying standards developed in Fourth Amendment jurisprudence.

Notice Requirements

1. Publication Notice: Rule G requires publication notice in newspapers and may require additional publication in specialized publications relevant to the property type or location.
2. Direct Notice: When the government knows or reasonably should know of parties with interests in the property, direct notice is required in addition to publication.
3. Notice Timing: Notice must be given promptly after property seizure, with specific deadlines for various notice methods to ensure constitutional adequacy.
4. Content Requirements: Notice must inform potential claimants of their rights, applicable deadlines, and procedures for contesting forfeiture.

Claim and Answer Procedures

Claim Filing Requirements

- Interested parties must file verified claims within specified deadlines
- Claims must describe the nature and extent of claimant's interest
- Claims must be served on the government attorney
- Late claims may be permitted for good cause shown

Government Answer

The government must file an answer to verified claims, creating adversarial proceedings similar to ordinary civil litigation.

Burden of Proof

After claimant establishes standing, government bears burden of proving property is subject to forfeiture by a preponderance of evidence.

Special Defenses

1. Innocent Owner Defense: Rule G accommodates innocent owner defenses available under various forfeiture statutes, requiring procedures for asserting and adjudicating these defenses.
2. Relation Back Doctrine: Forfeiture relates back to the time of the act giving rise to forfeiture, but innocent owner and other defenses may limit this principle.
3. Constitutional Defenses: Claimants may raise constitutional challenges including Eighth Amendment excessive fines claims and substantive due process arguments.

Disposition and Sale Procedures

1. Interlocutory Sales: Courts may order property sales before final judgment when preservation costs exceed property value or property is perishable.

2. Final Disposition: Upon forfeiture judgment, courts have broad authority to order property disposition, including transfer to government agencies, destruction of contraband, or sales with proceeds distribution.
3. Administrative Forfeiture Integration: Rule G coordinates with administrative forfeiture procedures, addressing cases where administrative forfeitures are challenged in federal court.

STRATEGIC PRACTICE CONSIDERATIONS

Jurisdictional Advantages

a) Forum Selection: Admiralty jurisdiction allows plaintiffs to choose from multiple potential forums based on property location, defendant presence, or contractual provisions.
b) Worldwide Service: Admiralty procedure permits worldwide service of process, expanding enforcement opportunities beyond conventional civil litigation limits.
c) Prejudgment Security: Attachment and arrest procedures provide prejudgment security unavailable in most civil cases, protecting against defendant insolvency or asset dissipation.

Risk Management

a) Security Requirements: Both plaintiffs and defendants must carefully evaluate security requirements and consider bonding costs in litigation strategy development.

b) Custody Responsibilities: Parties seeking arrest must be prepared for ongoing custody obligations that may exceed original claim amounts.
c) International Complications: Maritime cases frequently involve international elements requiring consideration of foreign law, treaties, and diplomatic implications.

Examination Focus Areas

a) Procedural Requirements: Students must understand the specific requirements for warrant applications, notice procedures, and claim filings that distinguish admiralty practice from general civil litigation.
b) Property Rights: Understanding the interaction between maritime liens, security interests, and ownership rights is essential for analyzing admiralty scenarios.
c) Jurisdictional Concepts: The relationship between admiralty jurisdiction, personal jurisdiction, and in rem jurisdiction creates complex analytical frameworks frequently tested on examinations.

The supplemental rules reflect admiralty law's distinctive procedural heritage while accommodating modern commercial and enforcement needs, making mastery of these specialized procedures essential for effective maritime and forfeiture practice.

Statutory Supplement

This statutory supplement provides essential federal statutes that work in conjunction with the Federal Rules of Civil Procedure to govern federal court jurisdiction, procedure, and practice. These statutes establish the foundational authority for federal courts to hear cases, define the scope of federal judicial power, and create substantive rights that influence procedural decisions. Understanding these statutory provisions is crucial for effective federal practice, as they often determine whether a case can be brought in federal court, which district has proper venue, and what procedural options are available. The statutes included here represent the most frequently encountered provisions in federal civil litigation, forming the statutory backbone that supports the procedural framework established by the Federal Rules.

28 U.S.C. § 1331. FEDERAL QUESTION JURISDICTION

"The district courts shall have original jurisdiction of all civil actions arising under the Constitution, laws, or treaties of the United States."

Core Requirements

Section 1331 establishes the fundamental basis for federal court subject matter jurisdiction over cases involving federal law, constitutional issues, and treaty disputes.

"Arising Under" Standard

The Supreme Court's interpretation in Louisville & Nashville Railroad Co. v. Mottley establishes that federal question jurisdiction requires the federal issue to appear on the face of a well-pleaded complaint, not merely in anticipated defenses or replies.

Well-Pleaded Complaint Rule

Plaintiffs cannot create federal jurisdiction by anticipating federal defenses. The federal question must be essential to the plaintiff's cause of action as stated in the complaint.

Constitutional vs. Statutory Jurisdiction

Section 1331 grants less than the full scope of Article III federal question jurisdiction, requiring that federal law create the cause of action or be a necessary element of the state law claim.

Practical Applications

1. Federal Cause of Action: Most straightforward application involves claims directly created by federal statute, such as civil rights actions under 42 U.S.C. § 1983, employment discrimination claims under Title VII, or antitrust violations.

2. Substantial Federal Question Doctrine: Some state law claims raise substantial federal questions sufficient for § 1331 jurisdiction when federal law is a necessary element of the state claim and the federal issue is substantial, contested, and capable of resolution without disrupting the federal-state balance.
3. Preemption Cases: When federal law completely preempts a state law claim, the claim is recharacterized as arising under federal law for jurisdictional purposes.

Strategic Considerations

1. Pleading Strategy: Careful complaint drafting can establish or avoid federal question jurisdiction depending on litigation goals and forum preferences.
2. Removal Implications: Section 1331 jurisdiction provides the basis for defendant removal under § 1441, making jurisdictional analysis crucial for removal strategy.

28 U.S.C. § 1332. DIVERSITY OF CITIZENSHIP JURISDICTION

"(a) The district courts shall have original jurisdiction of all civil actions where the matter in controversy exceeds the sum or value of $75,000, exclusive of interest and costs, and is between:

i) citizens of different States;

ii) citizens of a State and citizens or subjects of a foreign state..."

Diversity Requirements

Complete Diversity Rule

Strawbridge v. Curtiss establishes that no plaintiff may be a citizen of the same state as any defendant, requiring complete diversity among all parties.

Citizenship Determination

- Individuals: Citizenship determined by domicile, requiring both residence and intent to remain indefinitely
- Corporations: Citizens of incorporation state and principal place of business state under Hertz Corp. v. Friend
- Unincorporated Associations: Citizenship of all members determines association citizenship
- Legal Representatives: Representative's citizenship, not represented party's citizenship, controls

Amount in Controversy: $75,000 threshold must be satisfied exclusive of interest and costs. Plaintiff's good faith allegation controls unless legal certainty exists that recovery cannot exceed the jurisdictional minimum.

Practical Applications

1. Aggregation Rules: Single plaintiff may aggregate multiple claims against single defendant, but multiple plaintiffs generally cannot aggregate separate claims to meet the threshold.
2. Supplemental Claims: Once diversity jurisdiction is established, supplemental jurisdiction under § 1367 may allow related claims that lack independent jurisdictional basis.
3. Time of Determination: Diversity and amount in controversy are determined at the time of filing, with limited exceptions for post-filing changes.

Strategic Considerations

1. Forum Shopping: Diversity jurisdiction allows parties to choose between state and federal forums, creating strategic advantages in discovery, procedure, and substantive law application.
2. Removal Strategy: Diversity cases filed in state court may be removed to federal court, making citizenship and amount determinations crucial for removal analysis.

28 U.S.C. § 1367. SUPPLEMENTAL JURISDICTION

"(a) Except as provided in subsections (b) and (c) or as expressly provided otherwise by Federal statute, in any civil action of which the district courts have original jurisdiction, the district courts shall have supplemental jurisdiction over all other claims that are so related to claims in the action within such original jurisdiction that they form part of the same case or controversy under Article III of the United States Constitution."

Scope of Supplemental Jurisdiction

1. Same Case or Controversy Standard: Supplemental jurisdiction extends to claims arising from the same transaction, occurrence, or series of transactions or occurrences as the jurisdictionally sufficient claim.
2. Constitutional Foundation: Article III "case or controversy" requirement provides the outer boundary for supplemental jurisdiction, typically satisfied when claims share a common nucleus of operative fact.
3. Mandatory vs. Discretionary: Subsection (a) creates mandatory supplemental jurisdiction when requirements are met, subject to the limitations and discretionary factors in subsections (b) and (c).

Diversity Case Limitations (Subsection b)

1. Plaintiff Restrictions: In diversity cases, supplemental jurisdiction is limited for claims by plaintiffs against persons made parties under Rules 14, 19, 20, or 24, or over claims by persons proposed to be joined as plaintiffs under Rules 19 or 20.

2. Diversity Preservation: These limitations prevent plaintiffs from circumventing complete diversity requirements through supplemental jurisdiction.
3. Permissive Joinder Impact: Rule 20 permissive joinder of additional plaintiffs or defendants in diversity cases requires independent jurisdictional basis.

Discretionary Decline Factors (Subsection c)

Courts may decline supplemental jurisdiction when:

- Supplemental claim raises novel or complex state law issues
- Supplemental claim substantially predominates over federal claims
- Federal claims are dismissed
- Exceptional circumstances counsel against exercising jurisdiction

Strategic Applications

1. Claim Consolidation: Supplemental jurisdiction allows efficient resolution of related claims without requiring independent federal jurisdiction for each claim.
2. State Law Integration: Federal courts can resolve entire disputes involving both federal and state law claims when they arise from common facts.
3. Pendent Party Jurisdiction: Claims against additional parties may be heard under supplemental jurisdiction if

they satisfy the same transaction test and avoid subsection (b) limitations.

28 U.S.C. § 1441. REMOVAL OF CIVIL ACTIONS

"(a) Except as otherwise expressly provided by Congress, any civil action brought in a State court of which the district courts of the United States have original jurisdiction, may be removed by the defendant or the defendants, to the district court of the United States for the district and division embracing the place where such State court action is pending."

General Removal Requirements

1. Original Jurisdiction Prerequisite: Federal court must have original jurisdiction over the removed case, typically through federal question (§ 1331) or diversity (§ 1332) jurisdiction.
2. Defendant Right: Only defendants may remove; plaintiffs cannot remove their own cases from state to federal court.
3. Unanimity Rule: All defendants must consent to removal unless non-consenting defendants have not been served or would not be subject to personal jurisdiction in federal court.
4. Proper Federal District: Case must be removed to the federal district embracing the state court where the action is pending.

Diversity Removal Restrictions (Subsection b)

1. In-State Defendant Rule: Diversity cases cannot be removed if any defendant is a citizen of the state where the action is brought.
2. One-Year Limitation: Diversity cases generally cannot be removed more than one year after commencement, unless plaintiff acted in bad faith to prevent removal.
3. Fraudulent Joinder: Removal may be proper despite in-state defendants if they are fraudulently joined to defeat removal.

Procedural Requirements

1. 30-Day Deadline: Removal notice must be filed within 30 days of service of the removable document, typically the complaint.
2. Notice Contents: Removal notice must contain short statement of grounds for removal and be signed pursuant to Rule 11.
3. State Court Copy: Removal notice copy must be filed in state court with notice to all adverse parties.

Strategic Considerations

1. Timing Strategies: Defendants must carefully monitor service dates and case developments that might affect removability.

2. Waiver Concerns: Defendants waive removal rights by taking substantial defensive action in state court beyond seeking removal.
3. Remand Risks: Defective removal may result in remand with attorney fees and costs awarded to plaintiff.

28 U.S.C. § 1446. PROCEDURE FOR REMOVAL

Detailed Removal Procedures

1. Notice Filing: Removal accomplished by filing notice in federal court, not by motion or petition requiring judicial approval.
2. Automatic Effect: Removal is effective upon notice filing, automatically divesting state court of jurisdiction.
3. Bond Requirements: Most removals do not require bonds, though specific statutes may impose bonding requirements.

Time Calculation Rules

1. Service Trigger: 30-day period runs from service of removable document on each defendant individually.
2. Multiple Defendants: Each defendant has separate 30-day period from their service date, but later-served defendants cannot remove if earlier defendants' time has expired without removal.
3. Amended Pleading Removal: New 30-day period may commence when amended pleadings first make case removable.

Practical Applications

1. Document Review: Defendants must carefully analyze complaints and subsequent pleadings to identify removal opportunities and deadlines.
2. Coordination Requirements: Multi-defendant cases require coordination among defense counsel to ensure unanimous consent and timely filing.
3. State Procedure Integration: Removal intersects with state procedural deadlines, requiring knowledge of both state and federal timing requirements.

28 U.S.C. § 1391. VENUE IN CIVIL ACTIONS

General Venue Rules

1. Defendant Residence: Action may be brought in judicial district where any defendant resides, if all defendants reside in the same state.
2. Substantial Part Test: Action may be brought where a substantial part of events or omissions giving rise to the claim occurred, or substantial part of property that is subject of the action is situated.
3. Fallback Provision: If no district satisfies the above tests, venue is proper where any defendant is subject to personal jurisdiction.

Residence Definitions

1. Individual Residence: Judicial district where individual is domiciled.

2. Corporate Residence: Corporation resides in any judicial district where it is subject to personal jurisdiction at time action is commenced.
3. Unincorporated Entity Residence: Resides where it is subject to personal jurisdiction at commencement.

Strategic Applications

1. Multi-District Options: Venue rules often provide multiple proper districts, allowing strategic forum selection.
2. Transfer Considerations: Initial venue choice affects later transfer motions under §§ 1404 and 1406.
3. Personal Jurisdiction Intersection: Venue and personal jurisdiction requirements must both be satisfied for proper federal court action.

28 U.S.C. § 1404. CHANGE OF VENUE

Transfer Standards

1. Convenience and Justice: Courts may transfer to any district where action might have been brought for convenience of parties and witnesses and in interest of justice.
2. Alternative Forum Requirement: Transfer only to districts where plaintiff could have originally filed the action.
3. Discretionary Decision: Transfer decisions are discretionary, reviewed for abuse of discretion.

Balancing Factors

1. Private Interest Factors: Convenience of parties, witnesses, and sources of proof; availability of compulsory process; cost of attendance; practical considerations.
2. Public Interest Factors: Administrative difficulties, jury duty burdens, local interest in local controversies, familiarity with governing law.
3. Plaintiff's Choice: Plaintiff's forum choice receives substantial deference unless other factors strongly favor transfer.

Strategic Considerations

1. Timing of Motion: Transfer motions should generally be filed early in litigation to avoid waiver and minimize duplication of effort.
2. Law Application: Transfer under § 1404 requires application of transferor court's law in most circumstances.

28 U.S.C. § 1738. FULL FAITH AND CREDIT

State Judgment Recognition

Federal courts must give state court judgments the same preclusive effect they would receive in the rendering state, preventing relitigation of decided issues.

1. Claim Preclusion: Valid final state court judgments bar relitigation of same claims between same parties.
2. Issue Preclusion: State court determinations of contested issues prevent relitigation in federal proceedings.
3. Jurisdictional Prerequisites: State court must have had jurisdiction and provided adequate procedural protections for federal recognition.

Federal Court Applications

1. Defensive Use: Defendants may invoke § 1738 to prevent federal litigation of issues already decided in state court.
2. Jurisdictional Limits: Section 1738 does not create federal jurisdiction but affects how federal courts treat state judgments when jurisdiction otherwise exists.
3. Exception Recognition: Federal courts recognize limited exceptions for federal statutory rights that require uniform national application.

KEY INTERRELATIONSHIPS AND PRACTICE APPLICATIONS

Jurisdiction and Venue Coordination

1. Sequential Analysis: Courts must analyze subject matter jurisdiction, personal jurisdiction, and venue in sequence, as each presents different legal requirements and strategic considerations.

2. Removal Strategy: Sections 1331, 1332, 1441, and 1446 work together to create removal opportunities and deadlines that require careful coordination.
3. Supplemental Jurisdiction Integration: Section 1367 supplements primary jurisdiction grants in §§ 1331 and 1332, allowing comprehensive dispute resolution.

Strategic Forum Selection

1. Statutory Interaction: Understanding how these statutes interact allows effective forum selection and removal strategies that advance client interests.
2. Procedural Implications: Forum choice affects discovery rules, case management procedures, and substantive law application under Erie doctrine principles.

Examination and Bar Preparation Focus

1. Jurisdictional Analysis: Master systematic approach to analyzing subject matter jurisdiction, personal jurisdiction, and venue requirements.
2. Procedural Deadlines: Understand timing requirements for removal, transfer, and other jurisdictional challenges that create waiver risks.
3. Strategic Integration: Develop ability to analyze how statutory requirements affect case strategy and procedural choices throughout litigation.

These statutory provisions form the essential foundation for federal civil practice, working in conjunction with the Federal Rules to create the comprehensive framework governing federal court litigation.

References and Bibliography

PRIMARY SOURCES

United States Code Provisions

- 28 U.S.C. § 1331 (Federal Question Jurisdiction)
- 28 U.S.C. § 1332 (Diversity of Citizenship Jurisdiction)
- 28 U.S.C. § 1367 (Supplemental Jurisdiction)
- 28 U.S.C. § 1391 (Venue in Civil Actions)
- 28 U.S.C. § 1404 (Change of Venue)
- 28 U.S.C. § 1441 (Removal of Civil Actions)
- 28 U.S.C. § 1446 (Procedure for Removal)
- 28 U.S.C. § 1738 (Full Faith and Credit)
- 46 U.S.C. § 30501 et seq. (Limitation of Liability)
- 21 U.S.C. § 881 (Drug Forfeiture Statutes)
- 18 U.S.C. § 981 (Money Laundering Forfeiture)
- 19 U.S.C. § 1595a (Customs Forfeiture)
- 42 U.S.C. § 1983 (Civil Rights Actions)

Constitutional Provisions

- U.S. Const. art. III (Judicial Power)
- U.S. Const. amend. IV (Search and Seizure)
- U.S. Const. amend. VIII (Excessive Fines)
- U.S. Const. amend. XIV (Due Process and Equal Protection)

SUPREME COURT CASES

Jurisdictional Foundational Cases

- Louisville & Nashville Railroad Co. v. Mottley, 211 U.S. 149 (1908) (well-pleaded complaint rule)
- Strawbridge v. Curtiss, 7 U.S. (3 Cranch) 267 (1806) (complete diversity requirement)
- Hertz Corp. v. Friend, 559 U.S. 77 (2010) (corporate citizenship determination)
- Grable & Sons Metal Products, Inc. v. Darue Engineering & Manufacturing, 545 U.S. 308 (2005) (substantial federal question doctrine)

Personal Jurisdiction

- International Shoe Co. v. Washington, 326 U.S. 310 (1945) (minimum contacts framework)
- World-Wide Volkswagen Corp. v. Woodson, 444 U.S. 286 (1980) (foreseeability limits)
- Burger King Corp. v. Rudzewicz, 471 U.S. 462 (1985) (purposeful availment standard)
- J. McIntyre Machinery, Ltd. v. Nicastro, 564 U.S. 873 (2011) (stream of commerce doctrine)

Pleading Standards

- Conley v. Gibson, 355 U.S. 41 (1957) (traditional notice pleading standard)

- Bell Atlantic Corp. v. Twombly, 550 U.S. 544 (2007) (plausibility pleading standard)
- Ashcroft v. Iqbal, 556 U.S. 662 (2009) (plausibility standard application)

Rule 12 Motion Practice

- Hishon v. King & Spalding, 467 U.S. 69 (1984) (Rule 12(b)(6) standards)
- Davis v. Monroe County Board of Education, 526 U.S. 629 (1999) (motion to dismiss analysis)

Discovery

- Hickman v. Taylor, 329 U.S. 495 (1947) (attorney work product doctrine)
- Upjohn Co. v. United States, 449 U.S. 383 (1981) (attorney-client privilege scope)

Summary Judgment

- Celotex Corp. v. Catrett, 477 U.S. 317 (1986) (summary judgment trilogy)
- Anderson v. Liberty Lobby, Inc., 477 U.S. 242 (1986) (summary judgment trilogy)
- Matsushita Electric Industrial Co. v. Zenith Radio Corp., 475 U.S. 574 (1986) (summary judgment trilogy)

Class Actions

- Eisen v. Carlisle & Jacquelin, 417 U.S. 156 (1974) (notice requirements)
- Phillips Petroleum Co. v. Shutts, 472 U.S. 797 (1985) (absent class member rights)
- Amchem Products, Inc. v. Windsor, 521 U.S. 591 (1997) (settlement class certification)
- Ortiz v. Fibreboard Corp., 527 U.S. 815 (1999) (limited fund class actions)

Admiralty and Maritime

- The Moses Taylor, 71 U.S. (4 Wall.) 411 (1866) (admiralty jurisdiction scope)
- Executive Jet Aviation, Inc. v. City of Cleveland, 409 U.S. 249 (1972) (maritime nexus test)
- Norfolk Southern Railway Co. v. Kirby, 543 U.S. 14 (2004) (maritime contract interpretation)

Civil Forfeiture

- United States v. Bajakajian, 524 U.S. 321 (1998) (excessive fines analysis)
- United States v. Ursery, 518 U.S. 267 (1996) (civil vs. criminal forfeiture)

CIRCUIT COURT AUTHORITIES

Jurisdictional Issues

- Arbaugh v. Y&H Corp., 546 U.S. 500 (2006) (jurisdictional vs. merits determinations)
- Reed Elsevier, Inc. v. Muchnick, 559 U.S. 154 (2010) (subject matter jurisdiction waiver)

Venue and Transfer

- Piper Aircraft Co. v. Reyno, 454 U.S. 235 (1981) (forum non conveniens)
- Atlantic Marine Construction Co. v. U.S. District Court, 571 U.S. 49 (2013) (forum selection clauses and transfer)

Discovery Practice

- Zubulake v. UBS Warburg LLC, 217 F.R.D. 309 (S.D.N.Y. 2003) (electronic discovery cost-shifting)
- The Sedona Conference Cooperation Proclamation (discovery cooperation principles)

SECONDARY AUTHORITIES

Treatises and Practice Guides

- Wright, Charles Alan, Arthur R. Miller, Mary Kay Kane & Richard L. Marcus, Federal Practice and Procedure

(West Academic Publishing, multiple volumes and editions)

- Moore, James William, Moore's Federal Practice (LexisNexis, multiple volumes and editions)
- Friedenthal, Jack H., Mary Kay Kane & Arthur R. Miller, Civil Procedure (West Academic Publishing, 5th ed. 2015)
- Subrin, Stephen N., Martha L. Minow, Mark S. Brodin & Thomas O. Main, Civil Procedure: Doctrine, Practice, and Context (Wolters Kluwer, 5th ed. 2016)
- Yeazell, Stephen C. & Joanna C. Schwartz, Civil Procedure (Wolters Kluwer, 10th ed. 2019)

Admiralty and Maritime Law

- Schoenbaum, Thomas J., Admiralty and Maritime Law (West Academic Publishing, 6th ed. 2018)
- Force, Robert, Admiralty and Maritime Law (Federal Judicial Center, 2013)
- Robertson, David W. & Michael F. Sturley, Admiralty and Maritime Law in the United States: Cases and Materials (West Academic Publishing, 4th ed. 2016)

Civil Forfeiture

- Cassella, Stefan D., Asset Forfeiture Law in the United States (Juris Publishing, 2nd ed. 2013)

- Edgeworth, Dee, Asset Forfeiture: Practice and Procedure in State and Federal Courts (American Bar Association, 2nd ed. 2015)

Discovery Practice

- Ligon, John, E-Discovery: Law and Practice (American Bar Association, 3rd ed. 2020)
- Paul, George L. & Jason R. Baron, Information Inflation: Can the Legal System Adapt? (Richmond Journal of Law & Technology, 2007)

Class Action Practice

- Newberg, Herbert B. & Alba Conte, Newberg on Class Actions (Thomson Reuters, 5th ed. 2011)
- Rubenstein, William B., Newberg and Rubenstein on Class Actions (Thomson Reuters, 6th ed. 2020)

LEGAL PERIODICALS AND ARTICLES

Jurisdictional Analysis

- Burbank, Stephen B., The Class Action Fairness Act of 2005 in Historical Context: A Preliminary View, 156 U. Pa. L. Rev. 1439 (2008)
- Clermont, Kevin M. & Theodore Eisenberg, Exorcising the Evil of Forum-Shopping, 80 Cornell L. Rev. 1507 (1995)

Pleading Standards

- Miller, Arthur R., From Conley to Twombly to Iqbal: A Double Play on the Federal Rules of Civil Procedure, 60 Duke L.J. 1 (2010)
- Steinman, Adam N., The Pleading Problem, 62 Stan. L. Rev. 1293 (2010)

Discovery Reform

- Bone, Robert G., Civil Procedure: The Economics of Civil Procedure (Foundation Press, 2003)
- Subrin, Stephen N., Fishing Expeditions Allowed: The Historical Background of the 1938 Federal Discovery Rules, 39 B.C. L. Rev. 691 (1998)

Electronic Discovery

- Grimm, Paul W., Lisa Y. Bergstrom & Melissa M. O'Toole-Loureiro, Proportionality in the Post-Hoc World of Cost-Shifting for Electronic Discovery, 78 Geo. Wash. L. Rev. 465 (2010)
- Scheindlin, Shira A. & Jeffrey Rabkin, Electronic Discovery in Federal Civil Litigation: Is Rule 34 Up to the Task?, 41 B.C. L. Rev. 327 (2000)

COURT RULES AND LOCAL PRACTICES

Federal Court Local Rules

- Local Rules of Civil Procedure, U.S. District Court for the Southern District of New York
- Local Rules of Civil Procedure, U.S. District Court for the Central District of California
- Local Rules of Civil Procedure, U.S. District Court for the District of Delaware
- Local Admiralty Rules, U.S. District Court for the Eastern District of Louisiana

Advisory Committee Materials

- Advisory Committee Notes to Federal Rules of Civil Procedure (1937-2025)
- Federal Judicial Center, Manual for Complex Litigation (4th ed. 2004)
- Judicial Conference Committee on Rules of Practice and Procedure, Reports and Minutes (1935-2025)

PROFESSIONAL STANDARDS AND ETHICS

Model Rules of Professional Conduct

- American Bar Association, Model Rules of Professional Conduct (2020 ed.)
- Rule 1.1 (Competence)
- Rule 3.1 (Meritorious Claims and Contentions)
- Rule 3.4 (Fairness to Opposing Party and Counsel)

- Rule 11 Sanctions and Professional Responsibility Integration

Litigation Ethics

- Hazard, Geoffrey C. Jr. & W. William Hodes, The Law and Ethics of Lawyering (Foundation Press, 5th ed. 2013)

INTERNATIONAL AND COMPARATIVE MATERIALS

International Service and Discovery

- Hague Convention on the Service Abroad of Judicial and Extrajudicial Documents in Civil or Commercial Matters (1965)
- Hague Convention on the Taking of Evidence Abroad in Civil or Commercial Matters (1970)

Comparative Civil Procedure

- Zuckerman, Adrian A.S., Zuckerman on Civil Procedure: Principles of Practice (Sweet & Maxwell, 3rd ed. 2013)

ELECTRONIC RESOURCES AND DATABASES

Government Resources

- Federal Judicial Center (www.fjc.gov)

- Administrative Office of the U.S. Courts (www.uscourts.gov)
- Supreme Court of the United States (www.supremecourt.gov)

Professional Organizations

- American Bar Association Section of Litigation
- American College of Trial Lawyers
- International Association of Defense Counsel
- Maritime Law Association of the United States

Case Law Databases

- Westlaw (Thomson Reuters)
- Lexis (LexisNexis)
- Bloomberg Law
- Google Scholar
- Justia Free Case Law

BAR EXAMINATION PREPARATION MATERIALS

Commercial Preparation

- Barbri Bar Review, Civil Procedure (2025 ed.)
- Themis Bar Review, Civil Procedure (2025 ed.)
- Kaplan Bar Review, Civil Procedure (2025 ed.)

Academic Supplements

- Emanuel Law Outlines, Civil Procedure (Wolters Kluwer, 2025 ed.)
- Examples & Explanations, Civil Procedure (Wolters Kluwer, 8th ed. 2020)
- Glannon Guide to Civil Procedure, Learning Civil Procedure Through Multiple-Choice Questions and Analysis (Wolters Kluwer, 4th ed. 2018)

www.ingramcontent.com/pod-product-compliance
Lightning Source LLC
LaVergne TN
LVHW052025200926
848481LV00005B/1586
* 9 7 9 8 3 4 9 5 8 0 3 2 1 *